FIGHTING CPS

Guilty Until Proven Innocent of Child Protective Services' Charges

By Deborah K. Frontiera

The ABC's Press

Houston, Texas

2011

Bluebonnets Boots & Books
11010 Hanning Lane
Houston, TX 77041

13 Digit ISBN: 978-0-9800061-6-2
10 Digit ISBN: 0-9800061-6-3
Library of Congress # 2011903273

Note on the use of names: Any names used in this book are real names. Persons who contributed their experiences or their expertise and asked that their names not be revealed have designations which are obviously not real.

Project Coordinator—Rita Mills
www.booksconnectiononline.com
Editor—Faye Walker
Cover Design—Vicki Mark
Text Design—Rita Mills

The paper used in this publication meets the requirements of the American National Standard for Permanence of Paper for Printed Library Materials Z39.48-1984.
Printed in the United States

Dedication

This work is prayerfully dedicated to all the innocent: the children who are abused and the families of those wrongfully accused.

Thanks

The list of people who deserve to be thanked might fill a book by itself, and those people know who they are even if not named. But the author would like to recognize some special people: my publisher Rita Mills, my editor Faye, Mary Wright for additional encouragement and backing, all my family and friends for their constant prayers and encouragement during our ordeal, and those who contributed to Part Two and Part Three those named and those who wished to remain anonymous.

Table of Contents

Foreword

Deborah Frontiera's book is a case study in why crimes against children should be investigated by law enforcement as opposed to CPS a well-intentioned social service agency lacking law enforcement training, priorities and experience. As a direct consequence of CPS' misplaced priorities and inexperience, often poor investigations are conducted resulting in children being left in dangerous homes where they are re-abused, and, sometimes die.

The experience of our organization, Justice for Children, is that when investigations are done by the police, there is a much greater likelihood that the higher quality investigation will result in clearing the innocent and successfully prosecuting the guilty. While we espouse that the "system" should err in favor of the protection of a child, there is no doubt that children can be wrongfully removed from homes by CPS which can be traumatic to the child and their family. As stated by Ms. Frontiera about another case that had a successful outcome: "In this case, the initial investigation was done by a police officer, who knew the difference between discipline and abuse. It points to the possible advantage of having law enforcement, not CPS, conducting an investigation."

My hope is that this book will assist in our work for reforms to this system that fails children and families on both ends of the spectrum whether the home is dangerous or safe.

Randy Burton
Founder of Justice for Children

PART I

Our Family's Story

CHAPTER ONE

The Nightmare Begins

Saturday, April 14, 2007, around noon.

It wasn't a bad cell phone connection, but my daughter's voice faded in and out. "They're taking James away from us."

"What?" I couldn't believe what I was hearing. The evening before, my daughter had called to say they were going back to Texas Children's Hospital because "something" had shown up on our grandson's MRI. I had been worried, but there was nothing I could do about it. I was away from my home in Houston at a professional conference in San Antonio. I'd told my daughter to try not to worry, and since there didn't seem to be anything any of us could do that Friday evening, April 13, 2007, I'd told her to call me as soon as she knew what the problem was.

My daughter's voice shook as the phone call continued. "CPS is taking James away from us. They say we abused him!"

My mind flashed back to a conversation I'd had with a woman perhaps a year before about her daughter's experience and the battle they were still fighting to get custody of her granddaughter returned to her daughter. I remembered her warnings and advice to others: don't sign anything; document the day and time of every phone conversation; keep copies of everything . . .

"Rufina, no matter what happens, don't sign anything."

"Why?"

"It's too much to explain right now. Just don't sign anything."

I went on to say that I was on the way home, and her father and I would get up to the hospital as fast as we could. A few minutes later, my husband called. A caseworker was coming over to our house to talk about placing James in our care. Children's Protective Services likes to place children with family members whenever possible, my husband had been told. My mind was in far too much of a blur to remember much of the conversation later, but there was no doubt in our minds that we would take care of our grandson. I told my husband I'd be home in a couple of hours.

My hands ached from my tight grip around the steering wheel. Anger, fear, frustration, bewilderment every emotion possible coursed through me. I put my car on cruise control to keep from speeding.

Once I reached home, I dumped everything from my car onto our bed and my husband Jasper and I headed for Texas Children's Hospital.

"This guy, Derek somebody, came," my husband told me. "He took pictures of the house don't worry, I cleaned it up enough I told him I did not believe Rufina and Julio had ever abused James. He told me he didn't think it was abuse, but his supervisor might not agree. He implied that he'd had problems with his supervisor on other occasions. We have to go to court Monday morning."

"Which court?"

"The paper doesn't say; it just gives the address."

The rest of our conversation on the forty-five minute drive from our home in the northwest part of Houston to Texas Children's Hospital in the Medical Center Area south of downtown consisted of unanswered questions, what-is-going-on, I-don't-know . . .

The round of hugs when we arrived in James's hospital room was inadequate for our emotional state. Rufina tried to explain things she did not understand herself. Doctors and hospital staff refused to tell Rufina and Julio anything.

⫘

James had had his first seizure in February of 2007. Unexplained, no reason like a fall, a high fever, some new medication . . . It had happened at his babysitter's house. She had called our son-in-law immediately. Our son-in-law had taken James to his regular pediatrician the next day and the doctor was the one who formally diagnosed what had happened as a seizure. Dr. Isart had been James's pediatrician since birth. The size of James's head was always near the top of the charts but had not been a major concern. He was developing normally. The doctor told our son-in-law that it may have been an isolated incident, but he was not taking any chances. He referred James to a neurologist at Texas Children's. He also told Julio that if James had another seizure, to take him immediately to an emergency room.

When Dr. Isart called to book the appointment with the neurologist, the "next available" wasn't until May of 2007. A second seizure occurred on Feb. 20, 2007. Rufina and Julio took James to Cypress Fairbanks Medical Center not far from their home. A CT scan showed **no** injuries, **no** problems, nothing but a little sinusitis. However, that second seizure resulted in Texas Children's moving the neurologist appointment from May to March. At the intake appointment, the neurologist scheduled an EEG and an MRI. The EEG needed to be done "sleep deprived." At twenty-two months of age, James was very active, climbing anything he could climb, and he did not like to sit still. James's parents knew that the best way to keep James up was to take him somewhere with a lot to see. It happened that Julio's employer gave him tickets to an Astros' game the evening before the EEG, so we all went.

James spent most of the game running around the concession area under either Rufina's or Julio's watchful eye. Like all toddlers, James ran with his head leaning forward. His bigger-than-average head kept him unbalanced. He tended to fall down a lot. At the ball game, he got out of reach, fell forward and struck his head on the concrete floor at Minute Maid Park. It was quite a knot, but he quieted down after a few tears and was easily distracted.

The following morning, James seemed fine, except for being tired, of course. Rufina did not mention the knot on his head, and if the technician performing the EEG noticed it, he said nothing. April 10, 2007, Rufina had sent an email to family and friends. "I just heard from the pediatric neurologist. James's EEG came back abnormal, meaning he does have a tendency to have seizures, and they are starting him on anti-seizure medication. We still have to go to the MRI on Friday, but they do not think it will change their diagnosis."

There was a mix up in communication and the prescription for anti-seizure medication was not given to James's parents until the day of the MRI. The MRI on that Friday, April 13, 2007, had gone well. The technician had sent James and his parents off with the usual "we'll-call-you-with-the-results" parting.

Later that same afternoon, the hospital called Julio and asked him to return with the child and his mother, because "something" had shown up on the MRI and they needed to do more tests. Fearing cancer, or something unknown that might be worse, Julio left his job, picked up James from his babysitter, picked up Rufina from her job and continued the fight through heavy traffic on their way back to Texas Children's. The hospital called again wanting to know where they were, and they stated they were on their way and stuck in traffic.

They were told to go immediately to "Emergency" and someone there would direct them. They finally arrived around 4:30 PM. They were greeted in the emergency room with blank looks and told to wait. Two hours passed. No one would tell them anything. Julio found a snack machine, and James got a little something to eat. He ran across the tile floor, fell and struck his head on the tile floor of the waiting room in front of the security camera. When they were finally taken to an exam room, the nurse asked why they were there.

Rufina snapped an answer to the nurse that they were **told** to come there and that someone in the emergency room would **know.** They acted no different than any parents who had just received word that their child has the possibility of having some serious or possibly life-threatening disease.

"Are you okay?" the nurse asked. "You sound kind of 'reeeeer'."

Julio tried to remain calm and explained.

More waiting.

Finally, medical personnel told Rufina and Julio that the MRI showed blood spots on his brain and they wanted to do more tests. These tests included total body ex-rays, another CT scan, and a complete physical examination. Every doctor who came into their examining room searched James from head to toe for bruises, as if the other doctors might have missed something. The CT scan revealed two skull fractures.

Medical personnel asked Rufina and Julio only two questions: Had James been in a car accident recently? Had he fallen from a height of two stories or more? Of course, the answers to both were: no. Rufina and Julio told the doctor why they had come for the MRI, explained about the EEG ten days prior, and about the negative CT scan on February 20. They told the doctor about the fall on the tile floor in the waiting room and were told it was "too soon" for an injury from that fall to show up on their CT scan now. They were told, however, that the doctors couldn't tell how old the fractures were.

Months later I was still left wondering how they could make a statement like that. Why would a fracture not show up immediately on any X-ray or scan? Unknown to any of us at the time, a doctor named Michelle Lyn had looked at the MRI and ordered the second round of tests. She talked to Rufina and Julio only after the X-rays and CT scan, but only to say that the hospital social worker would be in to talk to them. We were not told at that time whether it was she, another doctor who also went off shift shortly after that, or the hospital social worker who called CPS. The signature on the affidavit was unclear and there was no printed name.

Rufina and Julio were told, still with no explanation, to continue to wait.

A young eye doctor came in and found blood behind James's right eye, asked no questions, and concluded the blood behind his eye was "consistent with a beating." He said that right in front of James's anxious parents. They then began to suspect what the extra tests were all about, but could not figure out why. They were told that the hospital wanted to keep James for observation. At 10:30 PM, James finally fell asleep.

At 1 AM, hospital staff told Julio and Rufina that they would bring in a bed so the exhausted parents could sleep. At 3 AM, after Julio had given up and returned to the waiting room to try to get some sleep in the chairs there, they finally brought the bed and told Rufina to try to sleep.

Julio's mother arrived at 9 AM with food for everyone. James ate eagerly, and Rufina and Julio tried to eat. A social worker, Derek Thorworth, arrived at 10AM to investigate. By 11 AM he told them that they were losing custody of James.

Julio held James tighter. Derek Thorworth said, "I'll be back in a little while." He seemed to sense Rufina and Julio were distraught. Perhaps he wanted to give them time to get used to the idea. When he came back, he asked Julio about possible family placement. Rufina was outside making phone calls to me and to her father. She had to leave the room so James wouldn't see her cry. They felt they had to be strong for James.

In an ironic way, the idea that CPS was taking James away from them was a relief. At least he didn't have cancer or another terminal illness. But at the same time, it was as if both their hearts had been ripped out.

Later, Julio told Rufina that he was thankful that he was holding James. Julio had always told Rufina that if anything ever happed to James or to her, the perpetrator better pray that the police found that person before Julio did. Holding James close to him kept him from lashing out at Mr. Thorworth and giving CPS a **real** reason to remove James from their custody. Julio never imagined that the ones hurting James would be an agency he couldn't touch, one that hid behind "Good Faith" laws.

Around 2 PM, James was finally moved to a room several floors up with surveillance cameras. Derek Thorworth came back at 3 PM after having been to our house. He handed them a piece of paper:

Notice of Removal of a Child *

* The italics in this section are Deborah Frontiera's.
Custodial or Absent Parent or Legal Guardian: <u>Rufina Bonilla</u>
Name or age and sex of child or children removed: *(blank)*
The Texas Department of Family and Protective Services (FPS) through its representative: <u>Derek Thorworth</u> took custody of your child or children: <u>James Bonilla</u> on *(blank)* at <u>3:45 PM</u>

This section is authorized by the Texas Family Code Chapter 262. We took the action because we believed:

1. The child's physical health or safety was in immediate danger, or the child was the victim of sexual abuse, or the parent or person with possession of the child is currently using a controlled substance and such use constitutes an immediate danger to the physical health and safety of the child;
    and

2. There was no time to obtain an emergency court order before the removal, or if an emergency court order was obtained, there was no time, consistent with the child's physical health and safety, for an advisory hearing.

    The facts that led us to believe the child should be taken into custody are: skull fracture and doctor's statements that it is consistent with abuse or neglect. The child will be placed with grandparents identified as Jasper and Debra *(spelling of my name was never corrected)* Frontiera.

    For information, you may contact: Name: Derek Thorworth **Office address and Day and Night telephone No.** 713-295-2500 **Documentation of Delivery:** "X" in the box of "Personal Delivery" I acknowledge that I received this Notice of Removal of Children on 4/14/07

    And the notation: "will not sign/refused"

"1200 Congress" was hand written at the bottom, the address of the Juvenile Court Building, but there were no further instructions.

Page two of the document read:

> **Child Safety and Evaluation and Plan**
> **Plan for Immediate and Short-Term Child Safety**
> **Family Name** Bonilla
> **Tasks and services**—List all tasks and services needed to provide for the child's immediate and short-term safety.
> **Family task:** child will reside with Jason *(arrow indicating correction to Jasper)* Frontiera at 11803 South Failhollow. *(incorrect address, not corrected)* The child will not be allowed to be in the presence of family babysitter. Pending Approval
> **CPS/Other service:** Work with services offered. Pending Approval

Beginning and ending Dates: 4/14/07 to *(left blank)*
Family Task: NA   **CPS/Other service:** NA
Beginning and ending dates: *(both blank)*
Method of Evaluation: NA

Conclusion-Identify plans for further services. When appropriate, describe the possible consequences if the family does not carry out this plan successfully. If the case is closed, explain why: Failure to comply could result in Removal. Pending Approval.

("The Signature of Parent" lines were, of course, blank.)
"The Signature of Worker" lines were signed by two people whose names were unreadable, with no printed names, and dated 4-14-07.
(The document above has been copied directly from the original in the possession of the author.)

———◆·◆◆·◆———

This document, with its many blank spaces, is how children are removed from their families in the State of Texas.

Friday night, April 13, 2007, behind the scenes, CPS had a doctor sign an affidavit, witnessed by a Notary Public, stating that James's injuries were "consistent with abuse/neglect." They hid behind the catch phrase "abuse/neglect" with the thinking that if the parents, or someone known to them, had not directly caused James's injuries, then the parents should have known the injury was serious and sought medical attention immediately, with the ability to explain how the injury occurred, and since they had not, they had "neglected" James. But how does one address an injury with no apparent symptoms? James had not lost consciousness, had not cried uncontrollably, had not been vomiting after the fall at the ball park or in the emergency room, had not had unequally dilated eyes, or other "classic" symptoms of concussion, then or at any other time previously.

It wasn't until June of 2009, when we inspected every letter every page of the court documents, that Rufina noticed a small but very important detail that we had all missed on the doctor's signed and notarized affidavit. The Notary Public had not dated it correctly, writing quite clearly **August** 13, 2007, not **April** 13, 2007. August 13 had, at the time signed, not come yet. Had we noticed this detail earlier, we could have contested the affidavit. Then the Court could have **compelled** the doctor to come to a hearing and verify her signature. (That Notary Public might have gotten in serious trouble, too.) If the doctor had then failed to show up, we could have pressed for the case to be dismissed immediately. However, in our wrecked emotional state of the moment, we didn't notice that important detail. We never were able to confront the doctor, our accuser, in court. Not one of the lawyers, CPS caseworkers, not even the judge, ever picked up on this, or if they did, they ignored it.

We knew we had to be in court Monday morning at 9:00 AM. How would we find a lawyer on a weekend? Our oldest daughter (a CPA working for a major Houston consulting firm) began making calls to her many contacts in the business world. The calls yielded one name of a lawyer who had expertise in Family Law and CPS cases. He wanted $15,000, and that was just for the retainer!

Rufina and Julio, still struggling under student loan debt and with only a few years in the professional work world, had very little in savings and essentially zero in home equity. Our oldest was in the process of purchasing her first house as a single professional. Our other married daughter and her husband were in about the same financial position as Rufina and Julio. Our youngest daughter was still borrowing money for college. Our own savings account, as two teachers raising four children and supplying the credit for their student loans, was more of a "put-and-take" account than true savings, and our retirement investments were in accounts we couldn't access without huge penalties. Julio's mother, single and working two jobs to support herself and Julio's younger brother who was still in high school, wouldn't be able to help pay a lawyer either. Short of winning the lottery or finding a tree with thousand dollar bills for leaves in our back yard, a $15K retainer was out of the question.

We dismissed the thought, each of us saying silent prayers.

I offered to stay with James in the hospital room so Rufina and Julio could go home, take a shower, and change clothes. They declined. Pacing would not help, so Jasper and I headed home, promising to return Sunday morning after church.

Feeling helpless, Julio and Rufina took turns pacing back and forth with James until he fell asleep. Then they tried to get some sleep themselves. Each time they closed their eyes, their brains relived the events of that horrible day. Over and over, they woke up in tears, feeling their hearts ripped out again and again.

•◦•◦•

Our friends at St. Catherine of Sienna Catholic church, where we had been parishioners since we bought our house in 1986 the same church where our youngest made her First Communion, where the girls had made their Confirmations, and where Rufina and Julio had been married could not believe what was happening to our family. My voice shook as I sang throughout the Mass. Fellow choir members offered their shoulders and echoed each other with offers to help in any way, especially with prayers. We went home feeling strengthened, changed clothes, collected what might be needed at the hospital, stopped at KFC for enough food to feed a small army for a day and headed back to Texas Children's. Julio's mother and younger brother were there as well. Hours get long in a hospital, especially with little sleep in the previous two days. Rufina and Julio had grown tired of the choices at a near-by McDonald's. James had not even been given meals by the hospital at that point. Everybody dove into the chicken.

We played with James, talked, tried to cheer each other up, and bit our lips trying not to cry, each of us trying to be strong for the others. A plan, even if we still had no lawyer, emerged. Rufina and Julio conceded that they would have to leave to get a change of clothes in order to be ready to go to court in the morning. Julio's mother said she would stay at the hospital with James during our court appearance. I suggested to my husband that he have Rufina and Julio drop him off at home while I stayed with James that evening. Rufina said she would bring some of James's toys, more diapers, etc. from home when she returned. Jasper would make calls to out-of-town family to let them know what was going on.

If I'm going to be doing this 24/7 for a while, I'd better get used to it, I thought after everyone left. James had dropped off to sleep, so I went to the hospital's play area on that floor and borrowed a few toys. I stared out the window until he woke up. Then we spent time sitting together on the floor while he experimented with ways to put the stacking cups together for forty-five minutes straight. His concentration on the task allowed me to see a different side of his personality than I usually saw an on-the-go toddler who climbed on anything he could and tried to run faster than his feet could go causing him to collect bumps and bruises like ants collect grains of sugar. Now I saw an intense little boy figuring out how everything worked, taking it apart, and trying the task again and again until he got it right. Fond memories of my girls at the same age flooded my mind. *It'll be fine like riding a bike. I remember being a full-time parent. I can do this,* I thought.

Rufina and Julio returned more hopeful. They might have a lawyer! While standing in the check-out line at a discount store, the woman ahead of them overheard their conversation. She said she had been through an ordeal with CPS and gave them her lawyer's number. She said he'd gotten her child back for her and was affordable. They had called, reached an answering machine and left an urgent message. We hugged our "good night," and I headed home promising to meet them at the courthouse in the morning.

❖

A call on my cell phone from an out-of-town friend bolstered my courage the next morning. Our conversation was full of righteous indignation toward "the powers that be." I'd sue that doctor when this was over with! Nail that guy to the wall for all this upheaval in our lives! But by the time I'd found a parking place, forked over more cash, walked the few blocks to the Juvenile Courthouse and gone through the metal detector, I felt very small again, wishing I had my husband with me. However, he had not been able to get a good substitute for his teaching assignment and figured both of us didn't need to be there. (I had called my favorite substitute Saturday evening and was thrilled that she was available for the full week.)

I had arrived at the courthouse early and realized I had no idea where I was supposed to go within the seven-plus story building. All we were told was "1200 Congress, 9:00 AM." I had rarely been to that area of downtown except for jury duty a couple of times, and that had been in a different court building. I clutched my purse and looked around for an "information" booth. There was none. The security people at the metal detector ignored me once I'd gone through.

A woman carrying a brief case came through security. I approached and asked if she could tell me where I should go for our type of hearing. She directed me to an office on an upper floor where we would need to get our "paperwork" before going to the seventh floor courtrooms. That paperwork would tell us which courtroom to enter. I called my daughter's cell phone to see how close she was and told her where I'd be. The paper work was not ready yet. I sat down on a hard, uncomfortable bench, examined my nails and put my teeth to work on a hangnail.

———•••———

When Rufina and Julio arrived, their faces reflected my anxiety. What if the lawyer didn't come? What were we supposed to do? Rufina, a CPA working for a firm with small business clients, was used to "professional dress," but Julio, manager trainee for a lumberyard, pulled at the tight collar of his dress shirt.

"James had four more seizures last night," Rufina said, "so it's not 'just at the sitter's house' any more. They are giving him a more of the medication than just the start-up amount. They won't be releasing him today." When Rufina ended up in tears after the fourth seizure, the doctor on duty during the night had rubbed her back. Over and over, it went through her head, "My child is having seizures, and they are taking him away form me! Why? Can I wake up now? Please, somebody pinch me so I can wake up."

A man probably not much older than my daughter and son-in-law got off the elevator. "Mr. and Mrs. Bonilla?"

"Yes."

"I got your message. I'm Frank Santulli. How may I help you?"

We had about fifteen minutes to try to explain the situation to the lawyer. He told us to relax, let him do the talking and, for the moment, agree to whatever CPS or the judge demanded. This hearing was mainly to formalize what we had already agreed to. There would be another hearing later where CPS would have to "show cause."

We went with him to the seventh floor and sat on another uncomfortable bench in the court room. Our lawyer scurried around along with several others, chatting in hushed tones, obviously at ease in his work place. Other people sat in the benches near us, staring ahead as we did, looking equally uncomfortable. The docket was called. We stood when the name "Bonilla" was called, then sat down to wait for our turn before Judge Glick. I tried to listen to what was going on with the cases ahead of ours, but the voices were too low to catch more than every fourth or fifth word. I did catch on to the fact that two of the cases involved severing parental rights and placing children for adoption.

We were called, stood before the judge, raised our right hands and swore to tell the truth. We each stated our full names and relationship to James.

"Are you married to this woman?" the judge asked Julio.

"Yes, Sir."

There were a few other questions. He thanked me for "stepping up to the plate" and then gave Rufina and Julio instructions: they were to make it as easy on Mom as they could; supply all diapers, etc.; keep James on their medical insurance; stay as long at our house as Mom and Dad say it's okay, but not over-night; complete everything and anything CPS asked them to do. They echoed "yes sir's" to each provision, their hearts sinking lower with each response. The judge set a date of April 25 for the "show cause" hearing.

That was it. Less than five minutes. Our grandson now "belonged" to the State of Texas and I was his primary care-taker. No place for "our" side of the story. No opportunity to ask questions. No opportunity to plead "not guilty."

We went back to the foyer on the first floor with Mr. Santulli where I called my credit card company to arrange a transfer of funds for a modest $2500 retainer, set up an appointment in the lawyer's office with both him and his legal assistant to give him further background and discuss strategy.

Rufina finally let out her tears in the ladies room. I reached for a pile of tissues in my purse, hugged her tight and reassured her that, no matter what, she was James's mother and always would be and nothing in this world could change that. We washed our faces with cool water and walked out of the courthouse with forced smiles.

"I've got to go over to my school and make some arrangements. Then I'll pack some things to stay with James at the hospital until he's discharged. I'll be up there by afternoon," I said. Rufina and Julio headed back for the hospital.

———•◦•◦•———

I managed not to fall apart until my principal had closed the door of her office. Then I burst into tears. The secretary handed me a box of tissues and both she and my principal rubbed my back until I was calm. I explained as much as I could.

"I think I should probably stay out the rest of the school year. I can't see trying to find a really good day care that will accept this whole situation easily," I stammered.

"Check the sick leave bank and see what Deb's got," my principal said to the secretary.

The secretary came back in a moment. "You've got plenty of leave. Don't give it a second thought. You've got Heather for this week and then we'll talk to Angie about long-term." She handed me the papers for "Emergency Family Medical Leave" and explained that at some point, and not to worry about it now, I'd have to have a doctor's signature on the appropriate line and turn the form in to the Personnel Department on or before the last day of the school year along with forms from CPS stating that I was James's primary caretaker. I said I'd try to come up occasionally to confer with the long-term sub on plans. I'd still need to do end-of-the-year report cards and paperwork but I could bring James with me to do those things.

I had always been careful about using my personal leave. The first several years of my teaching career, I'd used up each year's leave with sick children, etc. As the girls reached high school, I figured they could take care of themselves if they only had a cold and fever. Then my leave began to accumulate. After twenty-two years,

I had about eight weeks worth. It was my extra "insurance policy" so if I got in a serious car accident, needed surgery or something, I'd be able to stay out at full salary. (Even most short-term disability policies don't start to pay until after sixty days.) Well, here was that emergency, and I had the leave to do it.

Monday evening, Julio and Rufina stayed at the hospital until James was asleep for the night. He had been moved from the room with all the cameras to a "regular" room, one right near the nurses' station. Once I was there alone with James, they stopped checking on him so often. Perhaps they, too, made the assumption that my daughter and son-in-law were guilty. Certainly, that was the assumption the doctor signing the affidavit had made. I sat down with my journal and a new notebook, writing my deepest feelings in the journal and dates, times, people's names in the notebook. I had learned to document thoroughly as a teacher no "subjective" judgments, only observable behavior and facts. The journal would get my ranting and raving; the notebook would have "objective" material.

CHAPTER TWO

The "Investigative Phase"

The night from Monday, April 16, to the morning of April 17, 2007, was one of the longest of my life. James was wired up to a blood oxygen monitor because of turning blue during the seizures Sunday night. He was not allowed to leave the room unless we carried him. A sign on the door warned of the danger of falls. James woke during the night and when Grandma was the only one there, he was inconsolable. He wanted his mommy and daddy. No matter how much time he'd spent with me or the number of times he had happily stayed while Grandpa and I babysat for a couple of hours or half a day on a weekend, it was not me he wanted now. He pulled at the tubes, cried, and pushed me away, refusing my affection. I couldn't blame him.

The nurses only came in at the appointed times to check his vitals and he fought that, too. When he finally slept again, I tried to rest on the couch/bed in the room. Hospitals are not good places to sleep. There is always noise, and as soon as a person does manage to doze, someone comes in to check vitals again.

Every time an actual doctor came in, I tried to make a note of the name and ask questions. They were vague about answering and kept saying that everything would be in his records and I could request those later. I felt as though I, too, were regarded as some sort of untrustworthy person to be watched, guilty of defending my daughter if nothing else. Only James's neurologist, who had ordered the MRI and EEG originally, remained neutral.

I asked at least three doctors, including a neurosurgeon named Dr. Megahed (who was the emergency room neurosurgeon's "boss") if we should get James a helmet because he fell so often. The primary school where I taught had classes for the Pre-school Program for Children with Disabilities (PPCD). I worked closely with one of the PPCD teachers so her students and mine could develop friendships, a great benefit to all. One of her students wore a little helmet. I explained this to each person I asked. All the doctors I asked, and the nurses, said such a helmet would not be necessary for James.

When Rufina and Julio arrived at the hospital, their questions were ignored. Directions were given only to me. It was decided that James was stable enough to go home with me on Tuesday. I signed what seemed like a ream of discharge papers instructing me to make follow-up appointments with James's regular pediatrician, the eye doctor, the neurosurgeon, and his neurologist. Hospital staff made sure it was my car, with the proper child safety seat Rufina had brought with her, James got into and not his parents' vehicle. Rufina rode with me to reassure James while Julio followed us to our home with their vehicle. James was fussy; he'd picked up a cold virus in the hospital, and he wanted to go **home**, not to Grandma and Grandpa's house.

Thinking this would be very temporary, Rufina only brought a few toys and things James needed to our house. We would utilize the port-a-crib he was used to sleeping in when we babysat him instead of hauling over his full-size crib. We set it up in our youngest daughter's bedroom. She was away at college, and, surely, he'd be back with his parents before she returned home for the summer. We got James down for his afternoon nap; his parents went back to their jobs; and I settled down with the phone to book all the doctor appointments. I tried to convince myself, as our friends were saying, that this would be a precious time when we would have a special relationship with our grandson that we would not otherwise have. I convinced myself that we would be vindicated at the show cause hearing April 25.

That date reminded me that there were other things in my life I needed to address. My father would celebrate his ninetieth birthday on April 27. My brother and sisters and I had planned a large party at the retirement community where he lived in Florida. I was supposed to fly to Tampa on the April 25 to help make final arrangements and coordinate trips to and from the airport for the various arrivals, find out who had decided to rent a car and who would need a ride. I called one of my sisters to rearrange duties and the airline to change my non-refundable ticket to the April 26, agreeing to a hefty change fee. Then I wondered if I would have to cancel a trip to Denton that coming weekend April 21 where I was to attend a banquet for the North Texas Book Festival because one of my picture books was a finalist for their Children's Book Award. I decided not to call them until after we met with the lawyer the next day.

Did I have everything? Purse and loaded diaper bag—check. But did the diaper bag have a "sippy cup?" Did the cup have anything in it? Snacks? At least a couple of toys? This meeting with the lawyer was likely to last a while. I had forgotten how much stuff one has to carry around with a toddler!

"Come on, James, let's go pick up Mommy at her job." At the word Mommy, James eagerly hopped into his car seat and let me buckle him in.

Frank Santulli, his legal assistant, Julio, Rufina, James—running around in circles and then wanting to sit in a big chair like everybody else—and I sat around a conference table at the law firm office. After going over all the general information and background, Mr. Santulli wanted to talk to each of us separately. He was quite clear on the fact that he would be preparing us for the worst that could possibly happen.

I went first, taking James with me, because Rufina and Julio couldn't be "alone" with him, even if the secretaries and other office people were near by. They had their work to do and couldn't "supervise." James tried to play with everything within reach as we talked.

No, I didn't believe for a moment that either my daughter or son-in-law had abused James. Yes, I was in this for the "long haul" of six months to a year. But it couldn't possibly last that long, could it? The answer to that was vague. We were to be very careful. CPS could "drop in" at any time. Be sure to follow every rule they gave us, to the letter. Don't question. Don't argue. Don't show an attitude or anger. They would interpret any of these emotions in an unflattering light. Sarcasm or jokes would mean we were not serious, therefore not good "parents" and therefore not worthy of James being returned home. Showing anger would mean we all needed anger management classes and therefore were not "fit" parents. Let it play out "their" way, and James would eventually get back home.

Was CPS some sort of "Gestapo" group? Had a Communist dictator taken over the country and I somehow didn't notice?

I asked about my father's birthday party. Rufina had a non-refundable ticket, too.

"I advise you not to go."

"What! This is my father, Rufina's grandfather, James's great-grandfather's ninetieth birthday! How can they look on something like that in an unfavorable way?"

"They will look at it like this: she doesn't care about this child. She went off to Florida for four days to have fun."

I couldn't believe what I was hearing.

I explained about the North Texas Book Festival.

"That probably won't be a problem."

"Wait a minute here. It's okay for me to go to the awards banquet, but not okay to attend my father's birthday? The banquet is less of an issue for them than family?"

"I'm not saying I agree with this. I'm just telling you how they will view it. It's the distance. Hypothetically, if there were an emergency with James, you could leave Denton and drive back and be home in a few hours. All the way to Florida . . ."

"It's a five-hour drive from Denton. It's a three-hour flight to Tampa."

"That makes no difference in their eyes."

"What if I ask the caseworker?"

"I wouldn't do it."

Anger boiled inside me. I forced calm. How could this man sit there and tell me I should not go to my father's party!

While Rufina was with the lawyer, and Julio and I waited in the conference room with James, I needed to use the rest room. I asked a secretary where it was.

"Better take the baby with you," she said.

"Those are glass walls, for crying out loud. Can't you see through them? I'll just be a minute."

"Take him with you."

Had the entire world lost its common sense?

I went back, scooped up James and managed to fit him into the stall with me while I relieved myself.

The lawyer's sessions with Rufina and Julio were even worse. His questions seemed incredible to us, naïve as we were at the time. Are you prepared to divorce your husband/wife if it came out that your husband/wife was the cause of the danger to James? If it came to criminal charges against one of them, he would not be able to represent both. Were they prepared for that possibility? Any thought of Rufina going to her grandfather's ninetieth birthday was out of the question.

Rufina and Julio both signed releases so the lawyer could request medical records.

Deborah K. Frontiera

As we prepared to leave, he said again to me, "I know what you are going to do, but I still advise you **not** to go, especially you, Rufina."

My voice rose. "It's his ninetieth birthday, for God's sake!" James would have ridden on the plane free on Rufina's lap to see his great-grandfather for the first time.

"There's always next year."

"He's going to be **ninety**! There might not **be** a next year!" (I knew that only too well. My mother had passed away six weeks after celebrating her eightieth birthday in December of 2000.)

Furious, I scooped up James, turned and walked toward the elevator, biting the inside of my cheek to keep from screaming and almost screaming because I had to bite so hard to prevent a flood of tears.

We were silent until we reached the car. *Who knew? Maybe "Big Brother" had a bug somewhere near by.*

"It's okay, Mom. He's just doing his job. He has to tell us the worst. I'll stay home from Grandpa's party and help Dad so you can go."

Rufina said nothing more. She stared out the car window. Both of us knew we could not stop the tears if we tried to speak. Julio was silent, too. Even James was quiet.

———•◦•◦•———

The following morning, a different caseworker called to introduce herself. I asked to meet with her to go over the "ground rules." She couldn't get away from her office but would be able to meet with me if I could get there within the hour. Her office was thirty minutes away and James was taking a much-needed nap. Dilemma: take the appointment and wake a sleeping child into more crankiness or refuse and lose any chance I had of getting off on the right foot. I chose taking the appointment, hoping James would go back to sleep during the car ride.

Babery Fatema looked like she was younger than my daughter Rufina. I wondered if all her knowledge of how to raise children was "head" knowledge rather than practical experience. How can anyone who has never been around a sufficient number of children possibly give advice to parents on how to raise them? (I have a similar opinion of celibate priests conducting marriage counseling even though I am a faithful Roman Catholic.)

Ms. Fatema was pleasant enough as she explained that she had taken over the case form Derek Thorworth. I asked why there had been a change. She said Mr. Thorworth was the "initiating" caseworker. She would be our caseworker through the "investigative" stage. We would be assigned a third caseworker later to take us through our "service plan." She explained that an individualized "Family Plan" would be developed outlining the things our daughter and son-in-law would need to do to regain custody of their son. Each plan was supposedly tailored to a specific family. I was told that this plan would be ready within forty-five days.

I am familiar with different definitions of "days" so I asked if that meant forty-five business days (weekends not included) or calendar days. Ms. Fatema told me it meant forty-five calendar days. This meant we would know by May 28, 2007, (counted from April 14 when Mr. Thorworth presented Rufina and Julio with the first document) what this plan would entail; or May 30, 2007, if counted from the April 16 court date.

She asked me if I thought my daughter had ever abused James. I gave an emphatic, "No," and related a time Rufina had called me, frantic, "Mom, how do you put a band aid on the end of a tiny finger?" She had nipped James's finger when he wiggled while she was trying to trim his fingernails. I told her no band-aid would stay in place, just hold a tissue to it until it stopped bleeding.

"But how do I trim his nails?"

"Well, I just waited until you girls were asleep," I'd told her.

Ms. Fatema chuckled. She asked to take a picture of James. I allowed it. *Good rapport,* I thought, *bring up the trip.*

"Um, I need to ask about events coming up, but I don't want to 'break any rules' so to speak," I said.

"What do you need to know?"

I explained first about the book award in Denton. She congratulated me, two days and one night, not a problem at all. I told her about my father's birthday party, all the planning, that, of course, because of James's seizures, Rufina no longer considered taking him, or going herself . . . "It must be wonderful to have a father reach ninety in good health. Have a good trip," she said.

Well, she's not the boogey man after all, I told myself as she offered to carry James down to my car for me. I was glad of the offer. James still liked to be carried, but he was a big boy for his age. While I might have carried him with ease when I was my daughter's age, it was a different matter to my upper-fifties-age back.

On the drive home, my cynical side took over. Ms. Fatema may have only wanted to see that I had a proper child seat in my car. Babery Fatema never called our daughter or our son-in-law or visited their home. She never called his former babysitter or visited her childcare home. That interview seemed to be the extent of the CPS "investigation" into the alleged abuse/neglect of my grandson. In a criminal police investigation, police are obligated to check out an alibi. Apparently CPS does not consider it their duty to investigate. More likely, they do not have the time, the budget, or the necessary number of people on staff to conduct a thorough investigation.

James continued to cry himself to sleep every night after his parents left our house. Nothing any of us did could console him. Nothing could console Rufina and Julio either, as they had to leave their crying child behind every night, knowing he didn't understand, and neither did they.

Prior to going to the hospital, James had a good speaking vocabulary for his age. After being released from the hospital and coming to us, he had stopped talking, simply pointing and saying, "AAAAHHHHHH," for what he wanted.

—•◦•◦•—

We drove to the courthouse April 25, 2007, in a raging thunderstorm. Forecasters announced flash flood warnings over the radio throughout Harris County and stated that all flights from Bush Intercontinental Airport were grounded. Had I been at the airport at that time, my flight would not have left anyway.

I expected the hearing to be a sort of trial. I thought of Mr. Santulli as a "defense lawyer" who would question the CPS caseworker, the doctor who signed the affidavit (who never did attend any of the hearings) etc. I was naïve enough to think real court was like the scenes in television shows.

No family court judge wants the adverse publicity of sending a child back to parents when there might be even the slightest possibility of danger to that child. Only much later would we come to realize most family court judges were merely rubber stamps, doing whatever CPS wanted, shifting any possible "blame" away from them to CPS. Due to high profile cases in our area where children had died, CPS did not want adverse publicity either, so they were not about to send any child back to parents with even the slightest hint of danger. Since Ms. Fatima had not done any investigation and had not visited our daughter's home, she had no knowledge of whether James would be safe or not. In her mind, it was probably better to err on the side of caution.

The reality hit hard.

The hearing was nothing but a quick repeat of what took place on April 16. No questions, no comments, no chance to express "our" side. What follows is the entire text of Judge Glick's order, most of which was not stated during our brief time in front of his bench. The order follows a fill-in-the-blank format indicating that the same format is used for every case. Every item is always stated whether or not it applies to a specific case; and yet one must assume—to be on the safe side, and because so much goes unsaid—that each item applies to one's individual case even if an item isn't checked off. The italics are mine unless otherwise indicated.

DEREK THORWROTH 362-7
AIDA VILLARREAL 362-7
    CAUSE NO. _____200703616J_____
IN THE INTEREST OF IN THE DISTRICT COURT OF
    JAMES BONILLA HARRIS COUNTY, TEXAS
CHILD 315TH__ JUDICIAL DISTRICT
TEMPORARY ORDER FOLLOWING ADVERSARY HEARING

On_____April 25, 2007_____, a full adversary hearing pursuant to 262.201 or 262.205, Texas Family Code, was held in this cause.

1. **Appearances**
    1.1 The Department of Family and Protective Services ("the Department") appeared through **DEREK THORWORTH**, caseworker, and by attorney and announced ready.

    1.2 Respondent Mother **RUFINA BONILLA**
      __ appeared and announced ready.
      __ appeared through attorney of record
          _____ and announced ready.
      _x_ appeared in person and through attorney of record __Frank Santulli, III_____ and announced ready.
      __ waived issuance and service of citation by waiver and duly filed.
      __ agreed to the terms of this order as evidenced by signature below.
      __ although duly and properly notified, did not appear and wholly made default.
      __ was not notified, and did not appear.

(_x_ has been used where the actual form had a small box which was checked for the appropriate statement. The lawyer's name was hand written into the blank.)

1.3 Respondent Father **JULIO BONILLA**

The same choices and "x" and lawyer's name appeared as for the above.

1.4 Also appearing _____Deborah Frontiera and her Husband with the child_____
(The record of my appearance does not directly indicate that my husband and I were appointed by CPS as guardians.)

1.5 ____Jonas Hunter, Jr._____, appointed by the Court as *ad litem* of the child the subject of this suit, *(italics for "ad litem" appeared in the document)*
_x_ appeared and announced ready.
___ agreed to the terms of this order.
___ agreed to the terms of this order, but did not appear.
___ although duly and properly notified, did not appear.

2. **Jurisdiction**
   2.1 The Court, after examining the record and hearing the evidence and argument of counsel, finds that all necessary prerequisites of the law have been satisfied and that this Court has jurisdiction of this case and of all the parties.
   2.2 The Court further finds that the State of Texas has jurisdiction of this case pursuant to Subchapter C, Chapter 152, Texas Family Code, and because Texas was the home state of the child on the date of the commencement of this proceeding, and there is no prior child custody determination in another state.

3. **Findings**
   3.1 The Court finds there is sufficient evidence to satisfy a person of ordinary prudence and caution that: (1) there was a danger to the physical health or safety of the child which was caused by an act or failure to act of the person entitled to possession and for

Deborah K. Frontiera

the child to remain in the home is contrary to the welfare of the child; (2) the urgent need for protection required the immediate removal of the child and makes efforts to eliminate or prevent the child's removal impossible or unreasonable; and (3) notwithstanding reasonable efforts to eliminate the need for the child's removal and enable the child to return home, there is a substantial risk of a continuing danger if the child is returned home.

(Remember that no police ever investigated; no one ever talked to James's babysitter, his uncle, Julio's younger brother still in high school who lived with them, or Julio's mother who also lived with them. "Our" side was never presented in Court. Although Rufina and Julio had signed several releases of medical information by this point, medical records were not presented in Court because the opportunity to do so was not presented.)

> 3.2 The Court finds sufficient evidence to satisfy a person of ordinary prudence and caution that there is a continuing danger to the physical health or safety of the child and for the child to remain in the home is contrary to the welfare of the child.

> 3.3 The Court finds, pursuant to 42 U.S.C. Sections 671(a)(15) and 672(a)(1), with respect to the child **JAMES BONILLA**, that reasonable efforts consistent with the child's health and safety have been made by the Department to prevent or eliminate the need for removal of the child from the home and to make it possible for the child to return home, but that continuation in the home would be contrary to the welfare of the child.

(Considering that neither Rufina or Julio had ever been involved with the law other than minor traffic offenses, had no prior record of any involvement with CPS, and no case worker investigated their physical home, nor talked with them in depth about their lives or circumstances, I wondered what "reasonable efforts made" meant.)

> 3.4 The Court finds that placement of the child with the child's noncustodial

(my word processing program indicates noncustodial is not a correct spelling and prefers non-custodial, but the order did not insert a hyphen)

       parent or with a relative of the child is inappropriate and not in the best interest of the child.

(This statement also made me wonder because James had, indeed, been placed with relatives. So perhaps this finding did not apply because James's name had not been inserted as it had been in paragraph 3.3 above.)

    3.5 The Court finds that the following orders for the safety and welfare of the child are in the best interest of the child.

4.   **Appointment of Counsel for Parents or Parties**

    4.1 The Court finds that **RUFINA BONILLA** is/is not indigent. Based on the finding that **RUFINA BONILLA** is not indigent and pursuant to 107.015 of the Texas Family Code, **IT IS ORDERED** that **RUFINA BONILLA** IS RESPONSIBLE TO PAY A REASONABLE FEE IN THE AMOUNT SET BY THE Court by separate order to the attorney *ad litem* appointed to represent the child, **JAMES BONILLA.**

    4.2 The Court makes no finding with regard to the indigence of Respondent _____ because said Respondent is not presently before the Court and/or insufficient information is available to make such a determination at this time.

(This read the same as that above except that Julio Bonilla's name was inserted.)

5.   **Conservatorship** *(This word gets a "red line" from spell check, too.)*

    5.1 **IT IS ORDERED** that the Department of Family and Protective Services is appointed Temporary Managing Conservator of the following child:

        Name: **JAMES BONILLA**
        Sex: **MALE**

Birth Date: **JUNE 7, 2005**
Social Security Number: **UNKNOWN**

5.2 **IT IS ORDERED** that the Temporary Managing Conservator shall have all rights and duties set forth in 153.371, Texas Family Code.

    5.2.1 **IT IS ORDERED** that in addition to the rights and duties listed in 153.371, Texas Family Code, the Department is authorized to consent to medical care of the subject child, pursuant to 266.004, Texas Family Code.

OR

    The Court authorizes _____ to consent to medical care of the subject child, pursuant to 266.004(b)(1), Texas Family Code. This authorization is limited to the provision of medical care services appointed by the Medicaid program.

5.3 The Court finds that it is in the best interest of the child to limit the rights and duties of each parent appointed as a temporary possessory conservator. *(Spell check does not like the spelling of "possessory" either.)*

5.4 The Court makes no finding at this time with regard to the appointment of a Temporary Possessory Conservator.

(or)

    IT IS THEREFORE ORDERED that _____ is appointed Temporary Possessory Conservator of the child, **JAMES BONILLA**, with the limited rights and duties set forth below.

6. **Rights and Duties of Temporary Possessory Parents**
   6.1 Each Temporary Possessory Conservator appointed in this Order shall have the following rights:
   6.1.1 the right to receive information concerning the health, education, and welfare of the child;
   6.1.2 the right to access to [*sic*] medical, dental, psychological, and educational records of the child;

6.1.3　the right to consult with a physician, dentist, or psychologist of the child;

6.1.4　the right to consult with school officials concerning the child's welfare and educational status, including school activities;

6.1.5　the right, during times of unsupervised possession, to consent for the child to medical, dental, and surgical treatment during an emergency involving immediate danger to the health and safety of the child;

6.1.6　the right, during times of possession, to direct the moral and religious training of the child; and the right to _____

6.2　Each Temporary Possessory Conservator appointed in this Order shall have the following duties:

6.2.1　the duty, during periods of possession of the child which are not supervised by the Department or its designee, of care, control, protection, and reasonable discipline of the child;

6.2.2　the duty to support the child, including providing the child with clothing, food, and shelter during periods of possession of the child which are not supervised by the Department or its designee; and the duty to_____

(During the entire time that CPS was "Temporary Possessory Conservator" no caseworker ever accompanied us to any of James's many doctor or dental visits. I signed all the "permission to treat" forms. Neither my name, nor my husband's, is formally stated in this order as the person with whom James resided. No caseworker accompanied us when we chose James's Day Care Provider. Only once did a caseworker even stop by the Day Care Center, and that was after I had picked James up from the facility that particular day. The caseworker did not take the time to inspect the licensed facility, and never returned for a second visit.)

6.3　Possession of and access to the child

6.3.1 The Court finds that the application of the guidelines for possession of and access to the child, as set out in Subchapter F, Chapter 153, Texas Family Code, is not in the child's best interest. IT IS ORDERED that the parents named as temporary possessory conservators of the child shall have limited access to and possession of the child as set forth below.

The Court finds that the parents shall have the right to visitation with the child in accordance with the policy established by Department of Family and Protective Services and at all other times mutually agreeable to the Temporary Managing Conservator and the parents of said child.

(or)

IT IS ORDERED that each Temporary Possessory Conservator appointed in this Order shall have visitation with the child as follows:

(Several blank lines here)

7. **Child Support**

The Court finds that the parents have a duty to support the child the subject of this suit.

IT IS ORDERED that child support shall be paid as set out in Exhibit A attached hereto and incorporated fully herein.

(or)

The Court makes no finding at this time with regard to the payment of child support.

8. **Release of Medical and Mental Health Records**

IT IS ORDERED that Respondents **RUFINA BONILLA and JULIO BONILLA** execute an authorization for the release of Respondents', and the child's (if needed) past, current or future medical and mental health records to the Department from all physicians, psychologists, or other health care professionals, who have treated Respondents or their child with information the Department shall be authorized to share with all other groups or persons it deems necessary; and to further provide the Department with a list of the names, addresses of all physicians, psychologists, or other healthcare providers who have treated Respondents or the child. Respondents shall execute the authorization and deliver it, together with the list of physicians, psychologists, or other healthcare professionals, to the Department within 15 days of the date of this hearing.

(Rufina and Julio had already signed the releases, but had to sign them again—nd even again later on, because CPS could not find them.)

9. **Required Home Study**
   9.1 The Court finds that Respondent MOTHER **RUFINA BONILLA, has/has not** submitted the Child placement Resources Form required under 261.307, Texas Family Code.
   9.2 The Court finds that Respondent FATHER **JULIO BONILLA has/has not** submitted the Child Placement Resources Form required under 261.307, Texas Family Code.
   9.3 **IT IS ORDERED** that each parent, Alleged Father or Relative of the subject child before the court submit the Child Placement Resources Form provided under 261.307, if the form has not previously been provided (in effect for full adversary hearings that occur on or after November 1, 2005) and provide the Department and the Court the full name and current address or whereabouts and phone number of any and all relatives of the subject [*sic*] child the subject of this suit with whom the Department may place the subject child during the pendency of this suit, pursuant to 262.201, Texas Family Code.
   (My system doesn't like the spelling of "pendency")

10. **Compliance with Service Plan**
    10.1 **RUFINA BONILLA** is **ORDERED,** pursuant to 263.106, Texas Family Code, to comply with each requirement set out in the Department's original, or and amended, service plan during the pendency of this suit.
    10.2 **JULIO BONILLA** is **ORDERED,** pursuant to 263.106, Texas Family Code, to comply with each requirement set

Deborah K. Frontiera

out in the Department's original, or and amended, service plan during the pendency of this suit.

10.3 **IT IS FURTHER ORDERED** that:

(several blank lines here)

10.4 The Court finds that this order, as supplemented by the service plan to be approved at the Status Hearing under Texas Family Code 263.201, sufficiently defines the rights and duties of the parents of the child pursuant to Texas Family Code 153. 602 and satisfies the requirements of a parenting plan. To the extent there is evidence demonstrating that the child has been exposed to harmful parental conflict, the court orders that the Department address this issue in the Family Plan of Service.

11. Required Information

11.1 **IT IS ORDERED** that each Respondent to this cause provide to the Department and the Court, no later than thirty days from the date of this hearing, the information detailed below.

11.2 **IT IS ORDERED** that each Respondent to this cause provide to the Department and the Court the full name and current address or whereabouts and phone number of any absent parent of the child the subject of this suit, pursuant to Rule 194, Texas Rules of Civil Procedure.

11.3 **IT IS ORDERED** that each Respondent to this cause provide the Department and the Court the full name and current address or whereabouts and phone number of any relative of the child the subject of this suit with whom the Department may place the child the subject of this suit with whom the Department may place the child [sic] during the pendency of this suit, pursuant to Rule 197, Texas Rules of Civil Procedure, and 262.201(e), Texas Family Code.

11.4 **IT IS ORDERED** that each Parent furnish information sufficient to accurately identify that parent's net resources and ability to pay child support along with copies of income tax returns for the past two years, any financial statements, bank statements, and current pay stubs, pursuant to Rule

196, Texas Rules of Civil Procedure, and 154.182, Texas Family Code.

11.5 **IT IS ORDERED** that each Respondent provide the Department and the Court information sufficient to establish the parentage and immigration status of the child, including but not limited to marriage records, birth or death certificates, baptismal records, social security cards, records of lawful permanent residence ("green cards"), naturalization certificates, and any other Immigration and Naturalization Services records of lawful entry.

11.6 **IT IS ORDERED** that each Respondent provide the Department all information necessary to ensure the Department has an adequate medical history for the child, including but not limited to the immunization records for the child and the names and addresses of all physicians who have treated the child.

11.7 **IT IS ORDERED** that each Respondent provide the Department information regarding the medical history of the parent and the parent's ancestors on the medical history report form, pursuant to 161.2021, Texas Family Code.

11.8 **IT IS ORDERED** that each Respondent to this cause provide to the Department and the Court a current residence address and telephone number at which each can be contacted.

11.9 **IT IS ORDERED** that each Respondent to this cause notify the Department and the Court of any change in his or her residence address or telephone number within five (5) days of a change of address or telephone number.

12 **Dismissal Date and Notice of Status Hearing**
Pursuant to 263.306(11), Texas Family Code, the Court determines that the date for dismissal of this cause shall be _____ 4/21/08_____.

IT IS ORDERED that this cause is set for a Status Hearing, pursuant to 263.201 Texas Family Code, on _____6/08/07_ _____ at _____9:00 o'clock _a_m. in the

__315__ Judicial District Court of Harris County in Houston, Texas.

13. All said TEMPORARY ORDERS shall continue in force during the pendency of this suit or until further order of the Court.

SIGNED this __25th __day of ___April___, 2007.

_____

MASTER OF THE COURT

SIGNED this _____ day of _____, 2007

(April 26, 2007, was stamped in)

_____

JUDGE PRESIDING

(The signatures on the lines for Master of the Court and Judge Presiding are unreadable scribbles and no printed name is on the copy of the order that I requested. Note that neither my name, nor my husband's name, as the people caring for James, appear anywhere in this document.)
(The document above has been quoted directly from the copy given to the family by the court.)

———◆◆◆———

If this document seems complicated and confusing, remember it is the pattern for all such orders. At any point that our daughter and son-in-law failed to follow this order to the letter, CPS could press the Court to sever their parental rights and place James (or any child) for adoption either with another family member or with complete strangers.

If this is not frightening, it should be! A child may be removed from his/her parents on the basis of an anonymous phone call with no more investigation than in our case. CPS, with the full cooperation of the courts, has all the power. Parents have no rights whatsoever. They must comply or face the possibility of losing custody of their children permanently. That is the way the system worked against us, the way it works against many other families, the way it will continue until the public applies political pressure to change the law and therefore the way CPS operates.

After the hearing, Derek Thorworth asked to speak to Frank Santulli privately. Frank told us later that Mr. Thorworth indicated that he felt our case should never have been in court, that his supervisor insisted that he proceed to remove James from his parents' care even though he did not feel ours was a case of abuse or neglect. Unfortunately, as long as Mr. Thorworth was employed by CPS, he was unable to say that in court. James's parents had lost custody because of a power play by a supervisor over her caseworker.

———•◦•◦•———

That evening my frustration and anger boiled over. Tensions within the family swelled as my daughter and I set the table for dinner. James toddled around at thigh level demanding attention from everyone. My husband offered "advice" which, at the moment, I did not want to hear. Before I could say anything I would regret, I excused myself saying, "I need to go for a walk. Now!" I walked out the door and stomped my way around the block muttering expletives under my breath.

My daughters were born when I was twenty-one, twenty-five, twenty-seven and thirty years old. I had spent over a decade changing dirty diapers, being sleep deprived, taming two-year-old tempers, and doing all the other things that go with being a parent. I spent another two decades getting kids to school, going to PTA meetings, school carnivals, teacher conferences, sports practices and events, band concerts, etc. For all but six years, when I had the luxury of being a "mom at home," I had worked for a paycheck in addition to all the "mom duties." It wasn't that I regretted any of that. We had chosen to have four children and I knew I would be living my life for everybody but myself for the duration. I had no regrets there; I just wasn't anxious to repeat it. After so many years of no-time-for-me, I felt I had earned "me time." If that seems selfish to anyone, I make no excuses and refuse to feel guilty about it. My inclination when it came to people who talked about "empty nest syndrome" was to say, "Get a life!"

While my husband was supportive of our caring for James, I knew the bulk of the responsibility would fall to me, as it had when we raised our girls. Now, on top of my teaching job, and a second career of writing (which was beginning to take off) I had "motherhood" thrust upon me again. It was my choice to accept guardianship for my grandson; the alternative of having him end up in the foster care system was unthinkable. But it was not really a "choice" at all.

All of this bubbled to the surface as I trudged around the block working my arms back and forth at a fast aerobic pace fuming about "Big Brother" watching us all the time. By the time I had rounded the last curve and our house was in sight, the worst of my anger was spent. I re-entered the house and sat down with my family. "Sorry," I said. "I just had to blow off steam." No one said anything more about my outburst. It was the first of many quiet dinner times.

———◦•••◦———

CHAPTER THREE

Two Steps Forward, One Step Back

Between the two hearings, I managed to make the trip to Denton, for the North Texas Book Festival, but the situation at home was never far from my thoughts. I glanced at the face of my cell phone often, even though it was on "vibrate" most of the time. It felt dream-like when the banquet hostess called my name as the winner of the Children's Book Award. I floated from my place at one of the dinner tables to the podium. I remember vaguely saying how honored I felt and that receiving the award was a huge bright spot at that point in my life. Indeed, it was, but I wasn't about to explain my personal problems to a room full of strangers. When I got back to Houston, I put the framed award in a prominent place on the shelf in the "office" part of my bedroom. I'd look at it or just touch it whenever my emotions needed a lift.

While I was in Denton Friday night, Julio had had to work late to make up lost hours. Rufina was the one to put James to bed. She hoped he would fall asleep soon so she could slip out the door. Some forty-five minutes later when he was still awake, she realized that he would not let himself go to sleep when he knew she was leaving him. Holding back her tears, and knowing she had to leave so he would go to sleep, she walked out the door. She got into her car and bawled.

My father's birthday party gave me a different kind of strength that found in the absolute support of extended family. Even those who were not able to come were with me at heart. No family is perfect and my siblings and I had had our rivalries and spats as children. A lot of feelings had come up again when we had to divide up our mother's things after her death. My daughters had squabbled plenty when they were children and occasionally an old hurt would resurface. Sibling rivalry comes from instinct as animal groups act in ways that preserve the strongest of a species. Humans are animals, too. But in a crisis, families pull together. My family was there for me and my daughters were there for their sister, even though we are spread from coast to coast in states including Washington, Texas, Michigan, New York, Tennessee, Virginia, and Florida, with cousins, aunts and uncles in several more states.

Thursday evening, April 26, after a smooth flight to Tampa, I sat in my father's apartment with my oldest daughter, my brother and three sisters, brothers-in-law, cousins, several nieces, and closest friends from years and years back. I told our story to that point and listened to how-can-they-do-that and remarks about constitutionally protected legal rights, intrusive government, too many bureaucrats, what could they do to help, etc. I knew we were all one at heart and there was nothing in this world more valuable than that.

One sister announced that our dinner of meat pies called "pasties" was hot, so dig in. The "pasty" is an ethnic food particular to Michigan's Upper Peninsula where we grew up. A mixture of beef, potatoes, turnips, etc, wrapped in piecrust and baked, they originated in Cornwall, England but were adopted as the favorite food of every nationality of immigrants who worked in the copper and iron mines of the region during the early 1900s. What "Tex-Mex" is to a Texan, the pasty is to a Yooper (term for U.P.-er, or person from that region as opposed to "Trolls," or those who live "below the bridge" in Michigan's Lower Peninsula), and it would not be a family reunion of the Olson Clan without pasties. My sister had ordered enough for a small army from www.pasty.com, shipped frozen in dry ice and now hot out of the oven. I told everybody I'd said all I was going to say about CPS for the rest of the weekend and now I intended to have a good time.

The formal party took place Friday evening at the retirement community's club house. One brother-in-law had scanned photos my sister collected from all of us of my father clear back in his childhood, through his marriage to our mother during World War II, old black-and-whites from 1917 through new digital color shots with some of the great-grandchildren, ninety years of life. A rolling slide show of the photos played during the first part of the evening. We "roasted" my father with reminders of childhood goof-ups and confessions of sorts with much laughter. I presented my father with a T-shirt we had all signed which said, "Who are all these kids and why are they calling me Dad?"

The entire weekend helped me feel safe like a little child again, secure and loved unconditionally, accepted no matter what happened in my life. As we flew off to our homes all over the country, that was the strength I needed to return to Houston ready to face whatever happened and able to pass on the strength I received to my children and my grandson.

<hr />

Monday, April 29, Rufina and I took James to Dr. Isart, the pediatrician, for a late-afternoon appointment. (We'd asked for a time late in the day so Rufina could get in most of her workday before I picked her up.) He was shocked when we told him what had occurred while he was away on vacation. He told me how to be assertive in getting the medical records we needed from Cy-Fair. He also found, after measuring James's head again, that he was no longer in the ninety-five percent range, but was now above one hundred percent in head size for his age, weight and height. James's head had always been way above average, but this was the first time he had gone over the one hundred percent above normal mark. This concerned Dr. Isart, so he made a copy of the chart for us to take to Dr. Megahed. He indicated he would cooperate in anyway he could to help us through the ordeal.

Cypress-Fairbanks Medical Center, after looking at my driver's license, allowed me to have a copy of the February 20 written report on the basis of my name on the discharge papers from Texas Children's. They informed me the charge was around a dollar per page and was that okay? (Texas Children's could have gotten the copies for free—with the click of a mouse—but, to our knowledge, they had not requested them in spite of the signed release.) I gulped as I handed over nearly $30, almost all of my pocket money for the next two weeks.

Dr. Megahed's name fit him. I found him lacking in bedside manner and his tone of voice made it apparent that he felt the staff members at any other hospital were beneath him. "Well, it probably wasn't a pediatric radiologist who read the films," he said after glancing over the printed report from Cy-Fair at our appointment on May 3. "I'd really have to see the films to compare them." He glanced casually at the graph from Dr. Isart on James's head size, saying it couldn't possibly be correct, but his own measurement was exactly the same. His concern over the size of James's head seemed superficial.

When we persisted, he finally agreed to view the films, if I picked them up and brought them to his office, and agreed to do another CT scan to compare again a month or so down the road. I said I'd bring the films to our next appointment, which was two weeks later.

Getting the films from Cypress Fairbanks Medical Center entailed yet another trip out there. It is about a one hour drive between Texas Children's Hospital in the Medical Center area of Houston out to the Cypress Fairbanks area in northwest Harris County. During the drive, my mind wandered over and through many issues. Would I ever have an entire day at home so James and I could adjust to each other? Would requesting the films cost even more than the written report had? Did I have enough cash or would they take a check or credit card? It was beginning to feel like my entire relationship with my grandson would be spent talking to him over my shoulder as he sat buckled into his car seat while I drove around Houston.

I was pleasantly surprised to find there was no charge to check out the films. Even better, I didn't have to return them. The hospital's courier service would do that. So why couldn't, or wouldn't, Dr. Megahed request them himself?

Rufina and I were not prepared for Dr. Megahead's one-hundred-eighty degree change in attitude toward us during the next visit. He actually smiled at us, said, "I concur, there was no injury as of February 20, 2007." Many of our questions were finally answered. He handed us a prescription for the protective helmet I had asked about a month earlier. Yet, even then, he refused to get involved in the legal side or speak on our behalf to CPS.

His note in James's medical record (which I obtained later) read:

> **SUBJECTIVE:** James Bonilla returns to clinic. He brought a CT scan that was prior to the injury which was done at Cypress Fairbanks, and that was digitalized and reviewed for study. No evidence of fractures. He comes in with a follow up CT scan which shows that the subdurals are still there; but, he is clinically doing well despite the fact that he has a large head.
> **PLAN:** I am going to recommend to repeat the study. Hopefully these will resolve over a period of time. We are also going to get him a helmet because he has a tendency to fall.
> Hatem S. Megahed, M.D.
> Neurosurgery Service, HSM: MedQ/
> 284228494
> D: 05/21/2007 13:10:48   T: 05/22/2007 09:52:06

(Above quotation selected from medical records provided to the family by Texas Children's Hospital)

On the way home that day, as if I needed more stress, I looked over my right shoulder before making a lane change in stop and go rush hour traffic on the Katy Freeway. The truck in front of me stopped and I rear-ended him in my compact car. Five miles an hour, we didn't even so much as bump in our seatbelts, hardly a scratch to the truck's rear bumper. But my low front end went right under his jacked up bumper, causing major damage to my vehicle. The driver of the truck and I both drove away after exchanging insurance information. (I was glad we didn't need to summon tow trucks or police. I could not have handled a ticket for "following too closely.") I filed a claim on my comprehensive coverage and gave my insurance company the other driver's information. The owner of the truck never filed for damages. For the next three weeks, I drove various rentals and loaner cars while we shopped for a new vehicle. I would catch myself thinking *what vehicle am I driving today* as well as *where did I park?*

I went to a medical supply outlet the following day to get James's helmet. Neither Medicaid through the state (because James was in state custody) nor our daughter's private insurance covered it. I threw up my hands and pulled out my credit card. The woman in the office asked to see the Placement Papers to be sure I was authorized to fill the prescription. I explained I had not been given any. All I had was my name on the hospital discharge papers, and I didn't even have those with me. That led to explaining the situation. The woman said I should have gotten Placement Papers immediately; she knew because she was a foster parent. "Well, they haven't given me any," was all I could say. I explained our situation a bit more and she was shocked to find out that James had been removed so quickly.

She said that CPS is supposed to "work with a family" for a while before removing children from their parents.

"Not in our case," I said.

"Well that's not how they are supposed to do it," she said and handed me the charge slip to sign along with the helmet.

I called the caseworker when I got home, but I got only her voice mail. My call was not returned.

Gradually, our lives settled down. James and I began to develop a routine. I found that a neighbor cared for her granddaughter during the day, and we made a point to take walks together in the morning before it got too hot. A friend at church also babysat her grandchild and we arranged a play date. Each member of the family tried to find outlets for anger and frustration, and we avoided dumping on each other most of the time.

Early Childhood Intervention, totally unrelated to CPS, came to our house and did a complete developmental evaluation of James. Texas Children's had referred our case to them because of the seizure disorder. James had no developmental delays except for speech. Julio had been a "late talker" himself, and Rufina's younger sister had also had speech therapy as a child. It didn't seem to be a huge concern to us. James's regular neurologist thought speech therapy would be helpful and felt he was doing well on the seizure medication. The ophthalmologist declared James was fine, as far as he was concerned, and we didn't need to return to see him again.

I thought I might be a bit paranoid, but I continued to keep a notebook and jotted down every time James fell, anywhere in the house or away from the house, documenting the time of day, what he fell on, what part of his body might possibly have a bruise, what he was doing right before the fall, etc. My years as a teacher had taught me the value of proper documentation.

The Department of Family and Protective Services contracts with outside agencies to do portions of its background work. In our case, a group called the 4 C's (Children's Crisis Care Center) con-tacted Rufina and Julio to come in for a lengthy evaluation. For once, someone listened to their side, and more importantly, believed them! The woman evaluating their case said she usually had a shopping list of recommendations for CPS. For Julio and Rufina, she had only three recommendations: a psychological evaluation and parenting classes (which she knew CPS would insist upon anyway) and an interdisciplinary team to evaluate all of James's medical records since birth. It seemed as though everything might fall into place "for the good" after all.

May 23, 2007, was the scheduled day for the Permanency Planning Team Meeting. We expected to receive the "Family Plan" we had been told about earlier. I still had not received any Placement Papers. When I had managed to talk to anyone at the CPS office on the phone, all I heard was, "You haven't received Placement Papers yet? You should have gotten those right away." I felt like shouting, *"No, you idiot! Would I be calling to ask for them if I had gotten them?"* But I didn't.

The day started with a long drive to one of the CPS offices, this one on Murworth Sreet near the Astrodome (an even longer drive for me than Texas Children's Hospital). I had to take James there for 4Cs to do their evaluation of him before the afternoon PPT meeting. James was tired and cranky and not about to go with that strange woman in the office. I ended up having to stay in the room with him while the evaluator tried her best to get James to cooperate with her. He finally did relax enough to show her he was a typical almost-two-year-old who was "on target" developmentally except for language.

From the Murworth office, I drove to Texas Children's to pick up copies of his medical records, which I dropped off at my daughter's work place for her to make copies for CPS, 4Cs, our lawyer and the lawyer *ad litem*, then home where I fed James lunch and put him down for a short nap before driving back over to the Murworth office. The records from Cypress Fairbanks Medical Center proved that the seizures had come before the head injury. Those from Texas Children's included the notation from Dr. Megahed quoted previously.

The PPT meeting was attended by Rufina and Julio, their lawyer and his legal assistant, a moderator who did not work for CPS, the worker from 4Cs (the 4Cs staff had been the only truly helpful ones up to that point, and they do not work for CPS), a technician taking down the minutes, and Babery Fatema, the caseworker I had visited in April. When I expressed disappointment that the lawyer *ad litem* was not there, I was told he (or any lawyer assigned to be lawyer *ad litem* for a child) rarely attended such meetings. I found that strange, considering that he, as James's lawyer, was supposed to look out for James's best interests. He had seen James for less than ten minutes on the only visit he ever made to our home. How can anyone represent a child's best interests effectively when they never get to know that child's circumstances?

I later wondered why we had all bothered to give up our time. The meeting only reiterated what we already knew. Family reunification was the "permanency goal;" relative adoption was a concurrent goal; we should continue to follow up on all James's doctors' recommendations; CPS should obtain all his medical records and convene an Interdisciplinary Committee of doctors not connected with either CPS or Texas Children's Hospital; Rufina and Julio should both undergo psychological evaluations and attend parenting classes; our case should be referred to Child Advocates; we should follow all recommendations from Early Childhood Intervention concerning speech therapy.

The mediator who presides over the meeting, to make sure that everything that should be mentioned is mentioned, brought up the idea that "Munchausen's by proxy" (an emotional disorder in which a woman intentionally hurts her child or makes the child sick in order to gain attention for herself) should be looked into. At that time, we were dumfounded by that comment. Had James not gotten worse while he was in hospital care? Had he not turned blue from lack of oxygen while under the care of the doctors at Texas Children's Hospital? Rufina recalled the comment of the EMTs after his third seizure and **their** concern that James had not come out of the seizure quickly. Just because she knew the distance to five area hospitals shouldn't indicate that she was seeking to make her child sick to make herself feel better. Wouldn't any good parent know where hospitals were in case of emergency? Or, would a parent simply say, "Oh, no! My child has a broken arm. Where is a hospital?" Rufina could barely stand to watch James get his regular immunizations because she is terrified of needles. Why would she **want** IVs stuck in his arms when they had to prick him three or four times to find a vein? But no one ever asked Rufina these questions, and she was not given the opportunity defend herself on this topic at the PPT meeting.

Rufina handed the caseworker the copies of the medical records and was told our copies were not acceptable—something about "legal wording." When we asked for the family service plan, Ms. Fatima said sweetly that she had not completed it yet. (It had only been forty days.) I had asked our lawyer to be sure I got the Placement Papers. When he brought up the subject, the caseworker said she did not have them. I asked to speak and stated firmly that I was not leaving the meeting until I had **a piece of paper** I could turn in to the personnel office at Houston Independent School District, my employer. If I didn't turn in the proper paperwork for Emergency Family Medical Leave, my job would not be guaranteed when I would need to return to work in August. I could also have been denied portions of my salary for being absent all those work days without the proper paperwork.

Ms. Fatema's response was, "I'm not authorized to write anything like that." I was dumfounded. A supervisor attending the meeting by phone said she did have such authorization and told the caseworker to find an available computer in the building and write the letter.

Written on Texas Department of Family and Protective Services letterhead paper, it stated the following:

Texas Department of Family and Protective Services
1919 North Loop West, Suite 5
Houston, Texas, 77009
713-293-1800

To Whom It May Concern:

On April 14, 2007, James Bonilla was placed with his maternal grandparents, Mr. and Mrs. Frontiera. The Frontiera's (sic) are the primary caregivers of James. Although Chidlren's (*sic*) Protective Services currently has temporary custody of the child. (sic) Please contact the agency should you have any questions.
Sincerely,
Babery Fatema, CPS Investigator II

(This letter was copied directly from the original letter in the possession of the author.)

It is important to note here that the copy of the meeting form that we received states: "All information discussed at this meeting is to be treated as confidential and is not to be discussed outside of this meeting." Perhaps this is CPS's way of making sure the general public never knows exactly how they operate. This is why I decided to breach that confidentiality, with my daughter's permission and have included it.

Our daughter and son-in-law did everything asked of them well before all the deadlines given to them. We followed through on our part. Babery Fatema never did write the "Family Plan." She never requested the medical records in the format she had insisted upon. We never heard from CASA (Child Advocates) and when I tried to contact that agency to follow up, I was told that we would not be assigned to any of their Child Advocate volunteers unless it was "court ordered." The Interdisciplinary Team not connected with either CPS or Texas Children's was never convened. We never saw or heard from Babery Fatema or the supervisor attending the meeting by phone again. Months later, the letter quoted above was still all I had, and I was still asking for the Placement Papers.

CHAPTER FOUR

Going in Circles

May 24, 2007, I took James with me to my school so I could give the children in my pre-school class their Pre-kindergarten Completion Certificates and report cards and try to enjoy our last-day party. I was tackle-hugged by twenty-two four and recently-turned-five-year-olds. Their long-term sub stood back for an awkward moment. Young children have a strong bond with their first teacher. They had mourned and not understood why I was gone, but now I was back and they rejoiced. Then they had an odd look on their faces because they had also begun to form a bond with their long-term substitute and they might now have felt disloyal to her for embracing me. Together my sub and I regained gentle control.

The looks in their faces and their dual feelings for me and for my sub remained with me. I would see the same look repeated over and over on my grandson's face when he looked at my husband and me, and my daughter and son-in-law. In our case, CPS had not only disrupted an important bond between James and his parents; they had also needlessly disrupted twenty-two other young lives. The "you'll have a special bond with your grandson" line many friends had used to comfort us was that proverbial two-edged sword.

I had sent notes to the parents of my students in April to report that my grandson was ill and I needed to help take care of him, which was true, but I had confided the whole truth to only two parents, my "room mother" and another grandparent who had custody of her granddaughter for quite different reasons. Both had been supportive and kept the situation confidential. At that time, I didn't feel the rest was anybody's business. I centered my answers to questions on James's improving health, the medications he was taking to control the seizures and the reason for his helmet. All the kids thought his helmet was really cool and wanted to know if they could try it on.

That last day of pre-k or kindergarten was bitter-sweet, as it always has been for me. Kids are wild with the expectation of summer vacation. They also want to know if they will be in my class again the next year. Parents and I smiled and hid tears of joy that these children had grown and developed so much during the school year. It was both end and beginning, happy at the accomplishment and sad that our time together had ended.

James had a ball. The kids all wanted to help, invited him into every game and practically fought to help him up when he toppled over in the crush of little bodies. Thank goodness for that helmet and all the adults in the room. I stayed with them through lunch and had to pry myself away when it was time to leave. I had closure with this group of children, but not really. All of us would move on but with unfinished business haunting the back of our minds.

I buckled James back into his car seat and drove to HISD Central Administration to deliver a copy of the CPS letter that would let me return to work in August. James fell asleep in his car seat on the way. The parking lot was almost full and I ended up in an empty slot at least fifty yards from the entrance. James continued to sleep on my shoulder when I got him out. By the time I had carried him to the door, shifted him to my left to open the door, managed to present my ID badge, walked another twenty yards down a hall to the proper office, turned in the letter, and walked all the way back to my car, my arms were numb and my back was killing me. I'd need to call my chiropractor for an adjustment.

The following day, a teacher work day, I had James with me again as I filled out permanent records (James dragged out everything with wheels and every block in the room), sorted and put away materials (difficult to do with James still getting into everything and getting things out of boxes almost faster than I could put them in) and then tried to join my colleagues for the luncheon our Parent Teacher Organization always gives for teachers on our last work day each year. James was tired and cranky, wouldn't eat what I offered him, and generally let it be known loudly that he didn't like being restricted to his umbrella stroller or a booster seat at the table. I left early, hoping he would fall asleep on the way back to the school. He didn't. He wouldn't fall asleep on the pallet I put on the floor in a corner of the room as I tried to finish putting everything away for the summer. I gave up and let him play with anything that was still out and hurried to finish the job putting things anywhere they would fit into shelves and cupboards and figuring I would sort it all out in August.

That week of hectic activity brought out two needs: James needed to be around other children and stay on a regular nap schedule, and I needed more of a break than his naps provided. Even though school was out and my husband would be at home, too, I had other obligations—a signed contract with a new publisher for another picture book. My daughter and I discussed finding a daycare center and enrolling James a couple of days a week for the summer.

A friend at church gave me the names and phone numbers of two childcare centers, one a licensed home and the other a small Montessori school. The licensed home did not return my call. Ms. Patricia of Westwood Montessori urged us to come and visit. The children were outside playing in a tree-shaded, mostly grass, completely fenced playground that had a definite "back yard" feeling to it. The school was an older home, its rooms converted from living, dining and bedrooms to learn/play and sleep areas. James headed for a table overflowing with plastic building pieces the moment I set him down. I explained our situation to Ms. Patricia and asked if she was willing to take James, one, knowing CPS would be looking over her shoulder, and two, able to handle an emergency should he have a seizure. The answer to both questions was yes.

Rufina visited the school with me on her lunch hour a few days later. She had the same feeling of "welcome home" that I had. We decided to enroll James for the summer every Monday, Wednesday, and Friday, and full-time beginning the second week of August in case CPS had not let him return home.

My attitude improved immediately. I could have a leisurely lunch with a friend, wash the kitchen floor without worrying about James slipping on the wet tile, spend the day writing, or work on some free-lance editing I had picked up. It made up a little for the almost complete loss of freedom.

Eight years earlier, my husband and I had bought a "fixer-upper" piece of property in Michigan's Upper Peninsula not far from where I had grown up. Each year when we finished our teaching duties, we would head north on a two and a half day drive to spend the months of June and July working on it and recharging the batteries of our lives before facing another school year. It was on a small lake near the exit stream and marsh, surrounded by woods and only a few neighbors. We had named it the "Jade Retreat." Somewhere around a thousand hours of sweat equity had turned it into a lovely vacation home. It was highly unlikely that we would be able to go at all that summer. Court dates and doctor appointments were so close together that we didn't have two full weeks between them. Add to that the fact that we would have had to keep James completely away from both parents for that length of time because the judge's rule about no over-night stays at our house would prevent Rufina and Julio from traveling with us. We would also have to have CPS's permission to take him out of the jurisdiction. I mourned the loss of my annual retreat. The knowledge that I would have Monday, Wednesday and Friday between 9 AM and 4 PM made that loss easier to accept. And there was always the hope that, by some miracle, the judge would see CPS's error and let James return to his parents at our next court date.

We arrived at court on June 8, 2007, comfortably early. Our lawyer was early enough to have a quick conference before the docket was called. The forty-five days CPS had to deliver the "Family Plan" were up, but we had heard nothing. (The only contact since the Permanency Planning Team meeting had been a phone call to me from some secretary asking for the dates of James's various doctor visits.) The lawyer *ad litem* was present. No one from CPS was there for our case at docket call.

We sat. We waited. We waited some more. Our lawyer stepped out to talk to the lawyer *ad litem* to see if he knew what was going on. He didn't. We waited some more.

Someone made a phone call to try to see why no caseworker was present for our case. No one seemed to know. We waited again.

Past 11 AM, over two hours since the docket had been called, we received word that our caseworker had been "in an auto accident on her way to work." Our hearing was rescheduled for June 20, 2007.

We wondered why the caseworker had waited so long to say she could not come when it seemed it had not been a serious accident, but our lawyer said it was best to grant the benefit of the doubt. Our questions remained unasked, and therefore unanswered.

At this point, we decided it would be best to bring James's full-sized crib over to our house so he would get used to the idea that he might not go home for a while. After setting up the crib at our house, Rufina and Julio returned home to James's almost empty room. Neither of them could stand to see that emptiness, so they closed the door. Neither felt they would be able to open it again until their son returned home.

Rufina and Julio planned James's second birthday party for Saturday, June 9, two days after his actual birthday. The pizza and play place was noisy and crowded but the kids were having fun on all the little games and rides while parents and friends watched and tried to visit. Rufina and Julio had decided on a neutral location to spare us the confusion at our house. They didn't want to plan the party at their own home if CPS didn't return James because being at "home" might make James think he was home to stay. He might be even more confused and tearful when we had to take him back to Grandma and Grandpa's. In light of what had happened at court, it was a good thing they had planned that way.

We kept the conversation light and focused on the party and the kids, not our situation, and tried to enjoy the moment. Still, Rufina and Julio were unusually quiet when we loaded all the birthday gifts into our car, not theirs, at the end of the party. I'm not sure how she managed to keep her tears in check, but she did not let one tear fall where James could see it.

<hr />

I called Vanessa Thornton, whom we had been told was now our "service worker" on Monday, June 11, with questions about taking James to Brenham because it was outside Harris County (about an hour's drive northwest of Houston) and I wasn't sure at that point what the rules were. Rufina and Julio have close friends there (James's god father and his wife who had been Rufina's friend since grade school) and their son's birthday was coming up. On Wednesday, I left a second message, more urgent since that birthday party was now only a few days away.

Vanessa finally returned my call on Friday. No, Brenham was not a problem, she told me. Day trips were all right. Good, that meant we could take James to the beach at Galveston whenever we wanted as well. I asked about longer trips we were thinking about a one-week trip to Tennessee to visit our other daughter, her husband and our granddaughter. That required paperwork, Vanessa told me. She would send me the proper forms.

James had a regular check up with his pediatrician, Dr. Isart, on June 15. He was doing well. A second CT scan on June 18 showed everything was healing well. His head size was not quite on the chart but no longer as far "off the chart" as it had been in April. Dr. Megahed said he now felt James would "grow into his head size" and since James was doing well, we didn't need to make another appointment for six months. Early Childhood Intervention personnel did a complete developmental and language evaluation the following day at my home, and we decided on weekly developmental speech therapy sessions. The therapist could do them either at our home or at the daycare center if their appointment fell on Monday, Wednesday or Friday.

It took a couple more phone calls and a complaint to the Office of Consumer Affairs to obtain the travel forms from CPS. The Office of Consumer Affairs is the only place for people to complain about CPS actions, or inactions. They have no authority to enforce anything, or even do much beyond recording the complaint, but they at least listen and generally respond with a polite letter. Sometimes these complaints result in CPS doing at least the minimum required for a short time. When the travel forms finally arrived, I called to acknowledge receipt and was told that Vanessa was no longer working for CPS. Who, then, would come to court representing CPS on June 20? Would that person, if he or she showed up, have the long-awaited "Family Plan of Service?"

On June 19, a woman named Ms. Bonner called Rufina. "Do you speak Spanish?" was the first thing she said when my daughter answered.

"No, I speak English," Rufina replied. "My husband speaks both English and Spanish."

Ms. Bonner said that she was now our caseworker and asked Rufina if she was aware that we had a hearing the next day. (As if any of us could have forgotten it.) Rufina asked about the "Family Plan" and was told Vanessa (who had never talked to Rufina, Julio, or their attorney) had written it before leaving CPS. (But in the end, it had Ms. Bonner's name on it.) Ms. Cox, who was Ms. Bonner's supervisor, would take it to the courthouse because Ms. Bonner was going on vacation.

Rufina was exasperated at the assumption that she would need an English/Spanish interpreter simply because her last name was Bonilla. Hispanic last names are probably more common in Houston than any other ethnic name. Julio and his family had come to the United States legally when he was ten years old. While his mother still spoke more Spanish than English, Julio was fluent in both languages—a fact that gave him somewhat of an edge when it came to finding jobs in the Houston area. I calmed Rufina's insulted feelings by reminding her that many of the people CPS worked with locally probably did need interpreters.

"Yes, I know," Rufina said, "But if she'd **read** James's file, she'd know we spoke English."

<hr />

My cell phone rang around 8:45 AM as we were walking from a parking lot to the courthouse the morning of June 20, 2007. It was Ms. Cox. She had a quick question about James. After answering, I asked if we would be able to read the Family Plan before court. I asked if she had read James's file and she replied that she **had**. I said I was glad to hear that we'd be able to talk before court.

"Oh, I'm not there yet. I'm on my way," she said.

A nail embedded in our youngest daughter's sandal set off the metal detector as we entered the courthouse. (She was home from college for the summer and came to support her sister.) Jasper had to remove his belt buckle, but a four-inch pointed nail file in our oldest daughter's purse did not set off any alarms. They handed her purse back with no comments. The irony of that was our only humor for the day.

At 9:10, Mr. Hunter, the lawyer *ad litem*, called the court to say he was running a little late. Ms. Cox called in that she was "close." We waited once more.

I noticed that the same lawyers we had seen at other hearings were present again, even though the cases were all different. *Well*, I thought, *I suppose that makes sense to specialize.* That particular day, the cases we saw as we waited all seemed to be about severing parental rights of parents who, for whatever reasons, had not completed the requirements to regain custody of their children. It seemed to me that there were a lot of them and I wondered why. I could not quite hear any of the details because everyone standing in front of the judge spoke in hushed tones. From the benches where we waited, I could only catch every third or fourth word. Someone explained to me later that the reason for this is to "protect the privacy of the child." Only months later would I come to suspect that it also keeps the public from knowing how CPS operates, and that having the same lawyers on so many cases keeps things "all in the family." The bailiff was sure to hush those waiting for their cases to be called or people there watching if voices rose above hushed tones. If microphones are used in other types of court rooms so that everyone can hear, such devices were never in Family Court on any of the many occasions I was there.

Our lawyer had always given us stern warnings of the possible consequences if we ever arrived late for a hearing. He said that would be a definite mark against any parent trying to regain custody. Ms. Cox finally arrived at 9:55 AM and Mr. Hunter at 10:00. I wondered what Ms. Cox's and Mr. Hunter's definitions of "a little late" and "close" meant. The judge did not admonish them in any way for their tardiness.

The lawyers asked for a brief time so Rufina and Julio could be presented with "The Family Plan." The hearing lasted all of five minutes. Judge Glick asked CPS for their report. He asked the caseworker, not our daughter and son-in-law, if they had been given their Service Plan and if they understood it. Ms. Cox replied that she had given them the plan, and that they did understand it.

Our lawyer asked Ms. Cox if she had set up the Interdisciplinary Committee.

"What?" The look on her face made it only too obvious that she had not read the file or she would have known about that charge to CPS at the PPT meeting in May to set up such a committee.

Our lawyer also managed to get it into the record that we had waited an unduly long time for the Family Service Plan. He wanted to have a date set by the court by which CPS must obtain James's medical records and convene the Interdisciplinary Committee.

Judge Glick did not say anything to the caseworker about the length of time it had taken to get the Family Service Plan, but he set a mid-July date for them to get the medical records together. No one asked Rufina, or Julio, or any of the rest of us anything. Our next hearing date was set for October 29, 2007.

We retired to the hall outside the courtroom to confer. I asked Ms. Cox about the Placement Papers I still had not received.

"You don't have Placement Papers? You should have had those immediately."

I was beginning to become tired of that question and comment. "No, I don't have them, never have. This is all I have." I pulled out a copy of the letter I'd received in May. Ms. Cox promised to "look into it," and then she turned to leave.

Rufina and Julio emerged from a small conference room off the courtroom where their lawyer had taken them to go over the Family Service Plan. Mr. Santulli said he would try to get some items changed. Rufina wiped away a tear. Julio put his arm around her. She said, "So, the goal is to make sure we have all this done way before October." Mr. Santulli nodded and said he'd be in touch soon. He reminded them of his "score" with the judge and the fact that he saw that the judge noticed Ms. Cox's look of total dismay when he asked about the Interdisciplinary Committee.

My husband (always one for pessimism and worst case scenarios) rolled his eyes and muttered that he didn't believe a bit of it, that we had only wasted our time again. He couldn't see why all of us had to be there if we were not asked any questions and were not given any opportunities to speak. Our oldest and youngest daughters had wasted part of their work days for nothing. He said he did not plan to come the next time. Now we were definitely in this until at least October. I countered with my usual optimism, even though I was no where near ready to admit it out loud, I was beginning to think he was right.

Fury replaced any optimism when I read through the Family Service Plan! This long-awaited legal document, which we had been told was tailored individually to each family, was nothing but a cookie-cutter-one-size-fits-all, computer-generated paper with names inserted. This bit of writing, which we should have had within forty-five days, but which took them sixty-eight days to deliver to us, could not have taken more than twenty minutes to complete. In addition, the only places that could be individualized had numerous spelling and grammar errors; so it was apparent that no one had even taken the time to proofread it. As a teacher, familiar with how carefully special education documents for committee meetings and individual education programs must be done, and how completely free of any errors these must be, I found it shocking that such a sloppily done document would be placed before a court! *For crying out loud!* I thought. *CPS has computers to generate these things. Haven't they heard of "grammar check" and "spell check?"* I am quoting my daughter's entire plan below, exactly as it was written, errors and all. Julio's plan was exactly the same except that his name was inserted in all the proper blanks. The italics are mine.

Case Name: Rufina Bonilla   Case #: 26227389
FAMILY SERVICE PLAN
Cover Sheet I: Substitute Care
IDENTIFYING INFORMATION
Name of Parent(s)   **Date Plan Completed**
Rufina Bonilla   6/13/2007
Child(ren's) Name(s)   **Month/Year of Next Review**
James Bonilla   10/2007
PURPOSE OF THIS PLAN   To The Parent:
This is a very important document. Its purpose is to help you provide your child with a safe environment within the reasonable period specified in the plan. If you are unwilling or unable to provide your child with a safe environment, your parental and custodial duties and rights may be restricted or terminated or your child may not be returned to you. There will be a court hearing at which a judge will review this service plan.

If Judge Glick reviewed the plan, he never mentioned that fact when we were in his presence. In a later hearing, he only asked the caseworker, not our daughter or her husband, if the plan had been completed.

Child's Name   Long Range Goal for Permanency   Target Date
James Bonilla   Family Reunification   4/30/08

Goal Comments, only if necessary:
This portion was blank

EVALUATION OF PROGRESS
CPS will evaluate your progress with you on the basis of your successful achievement of the goals stated in this plan; your

successful completion of the tasks in this plan; and your ability to provide for the ongoing safety and well-being of your children.

Information for this evaluation may come from any of the following sources:
- you and members of your family;
- CPS staff who have worked with you;
- the initial report, or future reports of child abuse or neglect; and
- other agencies, individuals, and community professionals

Family Problems, Strengths and Changes Needed

LIST THE REASONS FOR CPS INVOLVEMENT:
On Saturday, April 14, 2007, DFPS received an intake alleging physical abuse of a one year old, James Bonilla. The intake alleged that the child has healing skull fractures and trauma to his brain.

LIST THE FAMILY STRENGTHS AND RESOURCES:
There are (*sic*) some family support.

SERVICE PLAN AND GOALS (sic) CHANGES NEEDED TO REDUCE RISK
What specific behavior(s) and condition(s) will demonstrate that the problems contributing to risk have been satisfactorily addressed and that the risk has been reduced?

Area of Concern: Child Vulnerability
Current Level of Concern: Considerable
Mrs. Bonilla will demonstrate the ability to maintain appropriate caregivers.
Mrs. Bonilla will demonstrate an understanding of and ability to support the child's special needs.
Mrs. Bonilla will recognize and accept the child's age appropriate behaviors and learn to cope with them.
Mrs. Bonilla will learn and understand the cause of the child's behavior.
Mrs. Bonilla will understand the child's limitations.

Deborah K. Frontiera

Mrs. Bonilla will demonstrate the willingness and ability to protect the child from harm.

Mrs. Bonilla will show the ability to parent and protect the child.

Area of Concern: Caregiver Capability

<u>Current Level of Concern</u>: Somewhat

Mrs. Bonilla will learn new behaviors that promote a positive self-image in the child.

Mrs. Bonilla will maintain a mature role model for the child.

Mrs. Bonilla will actively participate in therapy to understand how their own abuse/neglect as a child impacts their current parenting style.

Mrs. Bonilla will learn to exercise sufficient self-control to provide child with a sense of stability, fairness, and order.

Area of Concern: Quality of Care

<u>Current level of Concern</u>: Considerable

Mrs. Bonilla will demonstrate the ability to gain awareness of her own strengths, problems, and stressors in an effort to strengthen her family and make it a safe and protected environment for their (*sic*) physical and emotional growth.

Mrs. Bonilla will demonstrate the ability to provide child with adequate care and nurturance.

Mrs. Bonilla will demonstrate an ability to secure basic necessities such as food, clothing, shelter, medical care, and supervision for the child.

Mrs. Bonilla will provide food, shelter, clothing, and age related supervision for the child.

Mrs. Bonilla will demonstrate the ability to protect child from future abuse, and will show concern for child's future safety.

Area of Concern: Maltreatment Pattern

<u>Current Level of Concern</u>: Considerable

Mrs. Bonilla will learn and understand the adverse effects of substance abuse on herself and her child.

Mrs. Bonilla will maintain a drug free lifestyle and cultivate a circle of support away from drug abusers.

Mrs. Bonilla will properly care for the child to reduce the effects of drugs.

Mrs. Bonilla will demonstrate the ability to protect child from future abuse or neglect, and will show concern for child's future safety.

Mrs. Bonilla will demonstrate the ability to protect the child from future abuse, and will show concern for child's future safety.

*Considering that substance abuse had **never** been brought up in any of the allegations, or hearings, and our daughter (and son-in-law) had **no** history of any substance abuse, one wonders why this section was included in what was supposed to be an "individualized" plan. The fact that it is included, and the fact that the last two lines of this section are nearly identical, supports the idea that all "Family Service Plans" are identical, and therefore **not** individualized at all, or that the caseworker writing the plan had not checked into the case very thoroughly, if at all, or that both of these statements are true.*

Area of Concern: Home Environment
<u>Current Level of Concern</u>: Considerable

Mrs. Bonilla will maintain housing that is safe and free of environmental hazards and provide protection, food, and shelter for the child and family.

Mrs. Bonilla will demonstrate an ability to secure basic necessities such as food, shelter, medical care, and supervision for the child.

Mrs. Bonilla will learn appropriate ways to deal with stress in order to reduce the level of stress and chaos in the home.

Mrs. Bonilla will learn better ways to cope with stress.

Mrs. Bonilla will stop participating in criminal acts and accept responsibility for prior criminal activities.

Mrs. Bonilla will alter behaviors that expose the children to risk of harm.

*At the time the caseworker filled in the blanks in this document, **no one** from CPS had actually visited our daughter's home to see whether it was, or was not, safe. Neither our daughter nor her husband had ever had anything worse than a traffic ticket, so why was there a reference to "criminal activity?" Again, it shows the lack of investigation on the part* *of CPS. Background checks performed routinely by employers would have shown no criminal record. Why didn't CPS use even these simple tools before preparing this document that it took sixty-five days for them to complete? Or else, as stated previously, CPS has no such thing as "individualized" when it comes to "Family Service Plans."*

Area of Concern: Social Environment

Current Level of Concern: Considerable

Mrs. Bonilla will stop participating in criminal acts and accept responsibility for prior criminal activities.

Mrs. Bonilla will demonstrate the ability to avoid potentially abusive adult relationships.

Mrs. Bonilla will alter behaviors that expose the children to risk of harm.

Area of Concern: Response to Intervention

Current Level of Concern: Considerable

Mrs. Bonilla will demonstrate an ability to change the pattern of behaving that resulted in abuse/neglect.

Mrs. Bonilla will actively cooperate in fulfilling the agreed upon family plan of service in order to control the risk of abuse or neglect.

Mrs. Bonilla will demonstrate an understanding of how his/her own history has affected the care of the child.

Note the use of "his/her" in the sentence above, even after the "Mrs. Bonilla" at the beginning of the same sentence. It is another indicator that the entire plan is a computer-generated fill-in-the-name-blank document. Also, use of the terms "that resulted in abuse/neglect" shows the presumption of guilt, rather than a presumption of innocence.

EMERGENCY CONDITIONS

FPS has determined that one of the following emergency conditions continues to exist for this case and, therefore, services continue to be necessary:

1) A child is at risk of abuse or neglect, as determined by FPS;

2) A child has been removed from his/her home and placed in FPS care;

or

3) A child formerly in FPS care is at-risk of being returned to FPS care.

YOUR RIGHT TO REQUEST A REVIEW

You may request a review of this plan at any time. You may also request an administrative review or a fair hearing if CPS denies, reduces, or terminates protective services that you have requested, or does not act promptly on your request for protective services.

Rufina's lawyer said he would have the plan reviewed. To my knowledge, that never happened.

FAMILY SERVICE PLAN   **Tasks and Services for the Family**
Area of Concern: Child Vulnerability

The columns at the right: "Complete?" and "Court Ordered?" had boxes for a caseworker to fill in for each item. When the plan was given to our daughter, the "Complete?" column had "No" typed into each box. I was not able to see the caseworker's copy of the plan later to see if these columns were changed to "yes."

Task/Service   **Complete?**   **Court Ordered?**
INDIVIDUAL COUNSELING
Mrs. Bonilla will actively participate in couple weekly theraphy (*sic*) sessions to understand why she was unable/unwilling to provide the needed safety, structure, and supervision required by her limitations associated with their age& maturity level. (*sic*) Caseworker is referring the mother to Walker Counseling Associates. Mrs. Bonilla is responsible for contacting the therapist and scheduling her own weekly appointments for transportation. This service will be funded by CPS.
Parenting Class: Family Foundations
Mrs. Bonilla will attend, participate, and complete the six-week parenting class offered by Family Outreach to learn about her child's need for safety. She will need to demonstrate the ability to provide structure, stability, supervision & proper care to the young child.

Caseworker will provide her with handout detailing the information about the contact, location, and times of the service. The mother will provide the certificate of completion to the caseworker.

Area of Concern: Caregiver Capability   Task/Service
PSYCHOLOGICAL EVALUATION/TEST
Mrs. Bonilla will complete a psychological evaluation to be administered by Walker Counseling Associates to assess her emotional/mental health. She will need to follow all recommendations made by the therapist to address any issues of concern identified as a result of the test. Caseworker will contact the mother to provide her with date & time of the task. The costs associated with this service will be funded by CPS.

Area of Concern: Quality of Care   Task/Service
EMPLOYMENT/EDUCATIONAL/VOCATIONAL TRAINING
Mrs. Bonilla will need to maintain stable employment or demonstrate that she is enrolled in a vocational or educational training program to make herself more employable. Thus, enabling the mother to meet the child's basic needs. (*sic*) Mrs. Bonilla will provide the caseworker with monthly income statements to verify the legitimacy of the employment or copies of the enrollment papers to confirm her participation in a vocational or educational training program.

My daughter had already stated in court before the judge that she had a B.B.A. Degree in accounting and was a Certified Public Accountant working for a stable firm. Had the caseworker bothered to read the court papers, or James's file, she would have known that and this "task" would have been unnecessary. The fact that it is included shows, once again, that all the Family Plans are the same.

MAINTAIN APPROPRIATE HOUSING
Mrs. Bonilla will maintain suitable housing that is safe, clean, organized, with operational utilities and free of hazards to ensure James's wellbeing. Caseworker will make unannounced home visits to her residence to document progress in this area. Mrs. Bonilla is to provide copies of the lease/rent agreement to the caseworker no later

than by the 15days (*sic*) of her lease agreement. She is to contact the caseworker by phone or in person within 5 days of changing residence and provide the change in address.

VISITATION

Mrs. Bonilla will maintain contact with her children on a monthly basis to promote bonding/attachment. Caseworker will outline the conditions of the visits in a visitation plan. The mother must maintain a drug free lifestyle and provide two clean drug screenings before visits can be initiated. Testing positive for any illicit drugs will result in the visits being discontinued immediately.

*The judge had granted liberal visitation rights in our home on the very first "emergency" hearing in April. Our daughter and son-in-law's only restrictions were those that my husband and I imposed. The judge had only stated they could **not** stay at our home overnight. This section is another indication that the caseworker had not read the file and that all "Family Service Plans" are identical.*

Area of Concern: Maltreatment Pattern   Task/Service

Mrs. Bonilla will need to participate in weekly theraphy (*sic*) provided by Walker Counseling Associates to understand how her behaviors placed her children at risk. She will address why she has been unable to provide a stable home and drug-free home environment to the children. Mrs. Bonilla will need to demonstrate the application of skills learned through theraphy (*sic*)to change the behaviors that led to the abuse/neglect. Caseworker will arrange for services and communicate CPS concerns with therapist. Visits will be monitored between the mother and her child to assess her ability to learn recommended skills. Mrs. Bonilla is responsible for scheduling own weekly appointments with the therapist & make arrangements for transportation to and from the appointments. This service is funded by CPS.

Note that the word "therapy" has been misspelled three times. There are also earlier grammar errors, "there are some family support," and sentence fragments. Apparently, the caseworker, who supposedly has a B. A.

Degree in Social Work, was either unable to fill in a few blanks correctly, or failed to proofread the document before taking it to court. Granting her the benefit of the doubt, perhaps she is dyslexic. If so, she should have had someone proofread it. My dyslexic husband (who teaches advanced placement calculus at the high school level) always has me proofread anything he must turn in at work or for classes when he was working on his Master's Degree. Again, the use of the past tense in terms of abuse/ neglect points out the presumption of guilt, which was never proven, or even presented to a district attorney for possible prosecution.

Area of Concern: Home Environment   **Task/Service**
HOMEMAKING SKILLS
Mrs. Bonilla will need to learn to maintain housing that is safe, clean, and free of hazards to ensure that child's wellbeing. Caseworker will make unannounced home visits to her residence to document progress in this area. The utilities in the home must be operational, and the mother needs to demonstrate the ability to apply basic homemaking skills in her daily chores to include sweeping the floors, mopping, vacuming, *(sic)* dusting the furniture, washing dishes, and cleaning the bathroom & kitchen area. Caseworker will discuss progress with Mrs. Bonilla during the home visits and make recommendations for improvement.

When I typed in the word "vacuuming," my computer's word processing program auto-corrected it. I had to go back and intentionally spell it the way the caseworker had done it. We also wondered what CPS would use to gauge progress, since they had not talked to Rufina or Julio about any of this and had never visited their home to see what the "prior" conditions might have been.

CRIMINAL-FREE LIFESTYLE
Mrs. Bonilla will need to refrain from engaging in any illegal criminal charges or arrests throughout the course of this suit. She will need to stay in compliance with any court orders or instructions related to violations of the law to include probations, bail, parole, and community service. Caseworker will communicate with Law Enforcement to ensure compliance.

The first sentence in this task would be laughable if it weren't such a pathetic example of CPS' lack of investigation or checking with Houston Police Department. As previously stated, my daughter had never been charged with anything more than a minor traffic offense.

Area of Concern: Social Environment   Task/Service
AVOID DESTRUCTIVE NEGATIVE INFLUENCES
Mrs. Bonilla will stop associating or communicating with people engaging in self-destructive behaviors to include but not limited those with a history of drugs use and engaging in criminal activities. *(sic)* Caseworker will maintain communication with family to ensure compliance.

Here is yet another sentence lacking in proper grammar and punctuation and another example of CPS not checking with HPD for records.

SUPPORT SYSTEM
Mrs. Bonilla will develop and use a larger group of family for support. She will contact community resources to apply for and utilize the available resources that may benefit her family. Mrs. Bonilla will provide a list of these resources to the caseworker no later than 06/30/07 outlining the services available in her county to help meet the child's needs.

CPS had forty-five days to produce this document and did not meet their policy deadline. Our daughter had less than two weeks to complete this task. When she turned in the list of family and friends in her "support group," her list had twenty-eight people from our church, six immediate family members who lived in Houston, fifty-six friends in Houston, and thirty-seven family members and friends who lived "out of town." In-town family members had been to every hearing. I wonder what CPS was looking for in terms of "increase." None of the people Rufina listed were ever contacted by CPS.

Area of Concern: Response to Intervention   Task/Service
COOPERATION/PARTICIPATION/CONTACT WITH THE CASEWORKER

Mrs. Bonilla will follow all recommendations and/or services offered by the therapists, service providers, and CPS involved in her case to help eliminate the risk of harm to her child. The mother will contact the caseworker on a monthly basis a minimum of twice a month by phone, email, or in person to discuss progress made and any other issues of concern in completing the recommended tasks outlined in this service plan. The caseworker has provided Mrs. Bonilla with the contact information for the local CPS office.

PROVIDE OWN TRANSPORTATION

Mrs. Bonilla will make the necessary arrangements for transportation to ensure the timely completion of the tasks outlined in this service plan. Caseworker will be available to provide encouragement and discuss issues of concern with the mother on an outgoing (*sic*) basis.

Parent's Comments:

This box was empty because our daughter and son-in-law were given no opportunity to read or comment on the document before having to accept it in court.

Contact Person—For information about your children, please contact:

Name of Contact Person	Telephone
Kateika Bonner	713-940-5137 Ext

Beneath this (since Ms. Bonner was on vacation, and the former caseworker was no longer with CPS by the time we received the document) another name and phone were hand written on the document.

Georgia Cox	832-607- 6688

I (We) understand that I (we) can request interpreter or translator services if needed to assist me (us) in complying with this plan.

Rufina signed the document on 6/20/07. Ms. Bonner had signed it 6/14/07. A supervisor whose signature was unreadable (the letters in the signature

*did not look like those needed for "Georgia Cox") signed it 6/18/07,
errors and all.*

*(The document was copied exactly as written in the original which is now in the
possession of the author.)*

When Rufina began to make calls to schedule the psychological evaluation and counseling, Walker Counseling said they couldn't schedule an appointment because CPS had not sent them the necessary paperwork. The number CPS gave her for the parenting classes was not a working number.

———•◦•———

CHAPTER FIVE

A System Set Up for Failure

Rufina called me to get Ms. Cox's phone number because I had the notebook we had written it in the morning of June 20. She called Ms. Cox immediately to report that Walker Counseling needed the paperwork and that the number for the parenting classes was not working. That phone number was corrected by the end of the day. Friday, June 22, she called Walker Counseling again. They had received the paperwork, but this time the caseworker had forgotten to sign it. The woman at Walker Counseling called a supervisor, Mia Williams, to ask that the paper work be sent again, but got voice mail. Her call was not returned that day.

The following Monday, Rufina called Walker Counseling again to see if they had received the forms and was told the equivalent of, "Don't call us; we'll call you." When she tried to call CPS again, she opted to dial "operator" instead of the voice mail she'd been getting. The woman answering the "operator" menu number did not know anything, of course, but when Rufina left the message with her, the call was finally returned.

Later that day, CPS called Rufina's cell phone to try to speak to me to set up a home visit. I had given my number to several caseworkers or supervisors by this time, but somehow they didn't seem to have it. Rufina gave them my number. When a Ms. Aguilar called me, she asked if she could come by for the monthly home visit.

"Are you our caseworker now? What monthly visit?" I asked.

Ms. Aguilar said our regular caseworker was on vacation, and she was a substitute. She explained that the agency was supposed to visit children in foster care (or "kinship care" as in our case) once a month to see how a child was doing. This was now the third month of my caring for James and I told her no one had ever visited before. Ms. Aguilar seemed surprised to hear that.

When she arrived around 4 PM, she asked a few basic questions and asked to see where James slept. We had put the crib in our youngest daughter's room. Her queen-sized bed was there, too, for lack of any other place to put it. Ms. Aguilar (who could not have been over twenty-five years old) asked if anyone else slept in the room. I explained about the lack of storage space and said that no one else slept there. Our youngest daughter, home from college for the summer, was using the third bedroom, which my husband had converted into an office for himself once the older girls had moved out. We chatted casually. I learned that she knew absolutely nothing about our case and that her main job with CPS was to fill in when needed and transport children in foster care to doctor or dental appointments when their main caregivers, for whatever reason, could not.

She asked if I needed any advice on parenting skills. I asked if she had children; she didn't. I wondered how anyone so young, with no children of her own, with only "book knowledge" of how to handle children, could possibly offer advice to a grandmother who, in addition to four college-educated daughters, had also "raised" over four hundred kindergartners in twenty-two years, but I said nothing. She didn't know me, or our case, so I simply stated that I didn't think I'd need any advice. I asked about the travel forms we still had not received. She didn't know. She was the seventh person working for CPS (eighth if one counts the supervisor who attended the PPT meeting in May and authorized the letter for me to give HISD Personnel) to be involved with our case, none of whom seemed to communicate with each other or to have read the file.

She was a sweet young lady just trying to do her job. We never saw her again.

In spite of Walker Counseling's don't-call-us-we'll-call-you attitude, Rufina called them again on June 29. She was informed that her referral had been cancelled. Julio's still had no signature. Walker Counseling tried to call CPS (after all, their income comes from that agency) but CPS didn't return their call. Rufina called the CPS supervisor, who was "out of the office for the day." Rufina and Julio were responsible for making the appointments required in their Family Service Plan, but CPS, who required these appointments, was making it almost impossible to do so. She called her lawyer and the Office of Consumer Affairs.

Monday, July 2, Rufina finally reached Kateika Bonner, who was back from her vacation. She knew nothing about what had gone on in court, and nothing about the charge to CPS to set up an Interdisciplinary Committee of doctors to go over James's medical records since birth to see if they found any evidence of abuse or neglect. So she had not read the file at that point. She didn't know why I had not received the travel permits or why I still had no formal Placement Papers. But she promised to check into all of it.

By Thursday, July 5, Rufina was finally able to schedule the appointment for the psychological evaluation. It would take up most of her and Julio's work day on July 17. The Parenting Classes would begin July 20 and run for seven weeks every Friday from 9 to 11 AM. More time away from work for both of them. The agency doing the parenting classes told her she was lucky that was the last set of classes scheduled for "this year." Whether that meant the fiscal year, in which case a "new year" might begin August (many companies have the end of a fiscal year set for the end of July) or calendar year, we never found out. Still, the implication was that there would not have been another class available for quite some time.

Rufina and Julio's employers were very understanding of the situation and helped in every way to allow them to leave work when necessary. Julio had to make up the time by working a lot of Saturdays and Sundays or face a large cut in pay which they could not afford. Rufina knew (in her salaried position) she would not have any vacation or sick leave coming for another year.

I said a prayer of thanks again that I had accumulated so many personal leave days with my school district that I didn't have to worry. Making all my personal appointments during Christmas break, spring break or during the summer for so many years, and letting the girls take care of themselves once they reached their teens when they only had a cold was paying dividends now. I wondered if CPS would have considered me "neglectful" for that. But what is a working parent to do? People work because they need the income. "Unpaid" leave is not an option for the vast majority of families across the country these days.

The situation also made me wonder what a single mother with less than, or only a high school education, working for a less-understanding boss in a minimum wage job would do. CPS requires parents to maintain stable employment or enroll in some kind of training which usually doesn't allow a lot of absences. Yet the psychological evaluation they required was only offered during the work day. The parenting classes were also during the work day. What if a parent were fired for continually being absent from work? A parent might have to choose between the requirement of keeping a job, or the requirement of counseling and parenting classes. If they didn't do both, they could lose their children permanently. These requirements could create an impossible situation for many parents.

Was that why so many of the hearings we witnessed while waiting in court involved adoptions and severing parental rights? What happened to parents with less education than our family had who did not have the resources we had or the persistence to make calls in spite of don't-call-us-we'll-call-you attitudes we had encountered? What happened to those who could not afford lawyers but were "too rich" to qualify for a county-appointed attorney? A

Deborah K. Frontiera

lawyer *ad litem* is appointed for the child, but they do not represent the parent, nor do they help the parent. We had only seen James's attorney *ad litem* for about ten minutes outside the courtroom. How many families were caught in the same place we were, a narrow crevice between sheer rock cliffs created by CPS?

———◆———

Initially, my husband had been the cool-headed one, telling us all to keep calm and simply do what we needed to do to comply with CPS demands so James could go home. Now that it was clear that the situation would not be resolved quickly, he began to go through his "anger" stage. He can handle a lot, but he has does have limits. He felt an intense need to blame somebody. Unable to do that, he began to blame everybody. CPS was being stupid. Our daughter's lawyer wasn't doing enough. His "office" was now in the living room. James wouldn't leave his lap top computer alone. He had no privacy. We could never be alone. He was tired of "company" all the time. On and on. The stress was wearing on both of us.

One Friday afternoon while James was at day care, we thought we would escape to a matinee movie. Jasper went into complaining mode on the way to the theater. I had had enough and lashed back. Our argument grew so intense that I decided to get out of the car at the next stop light and walk home before I said something I would regret. He drove off. It was about four miles to walk home and Houston is not particularly pedestrian-friendly. I ended up calling our youngest daughter and asking her to come and get me.

Later my husband and I managed to talk it out. Sometimes he reminds me of the character in the movie *Ghost* who can't say "I love you" and substitutes "ditto." Jasper rarely says, "I'm sorry," but I can tell when he is. It boiled down to the fact that Jasper felt like a prisoner in his own home. He resented the fact that we had to live every day by someone else's schedule with no hope of regaining control of our lives. The explosion relieved the pressure that had built up in both of us and we talked about ways to relieve the stress it seemed we would be required to live with for the next several months. None of us had reached "acceptance." We were barely resigned to our situation.

Rufina and Julio were under even more stress than we were. Julio often stayed late at work in order to avoid the pain of watching his son interact with my husband instead of him. Sometimes he felt Rufina was taking "our" side rather than "his" on other matters. His mother had stopped by one day to visit James before she went to work, but instead of knocking, she had simply walked in, which my husband considered very rude. The first time, he had asked her politely to call first to be sure it was convenient for us, and to knock before entering the house. When it happened a second time, he yelled at her. She took offense at his yelling and said she would never enter our house again, for anything. That set off an argument between Rufina and Julio.

They were still not speaking to each other when they arrived at their next parenting class. Others in the class sensed something was wrong because Julio wasn't his usual "class clown" self. Humor was Julio's way of coping with the entire situation. Rufina could barely speak and ended up in tears. Never before had our family experienced such rifts, and it took a lot of understanding on everyone's part to forgive and move forward.

Julio had found a web site that discussed Children's Protective Services across the country. (www.fightcps.com) He brought it to Rufina's attention and she shared this helpful information with us. It concerned our lack of legal rights in the current situation and we learned about many of the rights we should have had. We also learned there were steps CPS would normally have followed (such as working with a family for a period of time before children were removed from a home) but these procedures had been cancelled due to CPS's use of an "emergency" order in our case. This meant that CPS had felt there had been a "clear and immediate danger" to a child, and it was their opinion that if they had not stepped in at that very moment, James would have been in mortal danger. CPS had started using "swoop and scoop" tactics. But we did still have some legal rights.

While CPS could indeed come to our home unannounced, we were not obligated to let them in unless they had a warrant. We had the right to say, "It's not a convenient time. Please come back later." The web site Julio found mentioned instances in which a woman was considered a "poor housekeeper" because dishes were soaking in a sink. Remember the provision in the Family Service Plan relating to a clean house? Dirty dishes could become a reason to consider the Family Plan unfulfilled. The site spoke of several cases where children were permanently removed for what seemed trivial things. I wasn't sure I believed everything posted on the site because these days, anyone can post almost anything on the internet and pass it off as truth. But it did help us rearrange our priorities. "It's not a convenient time" could allow for a lot of fast housecleaning. We also felt that phrase allowed us to stop having a "sitter" when we wanted an evening out. Our daughter and son-in-law could stay in our home and lock the door while we went out. They could call us immediately if anyone actually showed up. We also reasoned that if the caseworkers didn't have time to do the monthly visits they were **supposed** to do, they certainly didn't have time to drop in unannounced. Our paranoia began to disappear.

<hr />

Our travel permit finally arrived. We could legally take James on a one-week trip to eastern Tennessee to visit our other married daughter, son-in-law and granddaughter. It came with, finally, the Kinship Care information and detailed explanations of the process we had already been through, or had **not** been through because CPS hadn't followed the procedures laid out in their own information. It also described the processes we had yet to go through.

The Kinship Caregiver Agreement laid out the responsibilities of a family providing the type of care we were providing and the responsibilities of CPS. Among our responsibilities were:

> "work in partnership with DFPS . . . allow visits between
> child(ren) and parent only as approved by DFPS . . . provide
> food, shelter, clothing and other necessary supplies . . . if there is
> a need to take the child(ren) out of the county for more than 72
> hours obtain written approval from DFPS and the court . . . call
> DFPS about any emergency. . . not release child(ren) to the
> custody of any person, other than school personnel, day care
> personnel, or other persons involved in providing services . . .
> work with DFPS, and other persons to develop and achieve the
> child(ren)'s permanency plan . . . be available as a continuing
> placement for the child(ren) for at least six months . . . tell the
> child(ren)'s DFPS case worker about progress, visitors, and
> problems . . . cooperate with DFPS in removing any child from
> the home when DFPS decides such a removal is necessary . .
> . provide transportation for any medical and other necessary
> appointments . . . apply for any assistance for which the children
> might be eligible . . . arrange for child(ren) to attend school . . .
> keep all information about the children(ren)'s history of abuse/
> neglect confidential . . . not to discuss or tell anyone outside
> DFPS about the child(ren)'s history of abuse/neglect except
> when it is necessary to make sure the child(ren) receive
> appropriate educational, medical and therapeutic services, or to
> protect the health and safety of the child. . . participate in
> orientation, training, and other specialized kinship trainings . . .

comply with any other specific requirements or limitations that are set forth by DFPS or the court."

DFPS responsibilities were:
"provide casework supervision . . . investigate all allegations of abuse and neglect . . . keep the kinship caregiver informed of a ny changes . . . develop with the kinship caregiver a 'plan of service' . . . provide known health and educational information . . . inform the kinship caregiver about any public assistance programs that may be available to assist the kinship caregiver in applying for public assistance for the children."

(The portions of the "Kindship Caregiver Agreement" quoted here have been edited to include the most pertinent aspects. The author has possession of the entire original document.)

The packet also said that while there would be no monthly financial compensation (as there would be for a foster family) for Kinship caregivers, there was a one-time allowance of $1000 for a family to offset the financial burden. Supposedly, I'd also be eligible for CPS to pay the daycare center when I returned to work in August. But to qualify for any of these benefits, a family's income level could be no more than 300% of the poverty level as defined by federal poverty guidelines. That left us out. Once again, as members of the middle class, we were "too rich" to qualify for help. We had all of the responsibility, all of the cost, but none of the parental rights.

I had already broken the confidentiality requirement with my constant communications to family and friends both in and out of town. We were never consulted about, or asked to participate in, any "plan of service" or any training sessions. The only service CPS ever provided was to send us a Medicaid card and inform us that we could apply for Women Infants and Children. The WIC coupons provided about $55 a month in milk, cereal, fruit juice, eggs, cheese, and dried beans or peanut butter not much, but more help than we had been getting.

⋯

Sunday, July 15, we finally managed to take a day-trip to our favorite beach park in Galveston. Jasper and I had taken a "scouting trip" a few days before to make sure the park had reopened (it had been closed for several months for renovation) and to see how James would react to a longer drive in the car with us— preparation for the trip to Tennessee. The park had reopened with even nicer facilities: restrooms with showers, deck with picnic tables and a board walk over the dunes to the beach area. The park now sat in the shadow of a high-rise condo hotel and shared its driveway, so few people realized it was open again. There were almost no other people that day. Besides ourselves and Rufina and Julio, his mother came and brought the youngest of her other grandchildren (a daughter of Julio's older sister). It was cloudy so we didn't need a beach umbrella. We swam, relaxed, flew James's kite with him, blew bubbles, built a sand castle . . . all the fun things families do at a beach. We drove home tired and happy, and James slept well.

⋯

Rufina and Julio's psychological evaluations had been set for July 17. Both had arranged for half a day off from their jobs, but on July 16, Walker Counseling still had not received the Julio's paperwork from CPS. Rufina called the CPS office again and stated bluntly, "Look, we can't afford to take half a day off for nothing!" She got a promise that it would be faxed that day, but 4 PM came and went with no fax. By some miracle, the paperwork was there when they arrived at Walker Counseling. The evaluation took place as scheduled.

Deborah K. Frontiera

Over the next two weeks (July 19, 20, 24, and 25) Rufina or I left messages with CPS asking about the progress of setting up the Interdisciplinary Committee. None of the calls were returned. A supervisor finally called on July 31 and asked Rufina, "Tell me, why we are doing this Interdisciplinary Committee?"

Rufina wanted to shout, *"If you would read the file, you would know!"* But she refrained and explained, again, what had taken place at the PPT meeting in May and during Court in June. **Again**, she gave the CPS supervisor the names of every doctor and hospital involved since James's birth. The supervisor also said that our caseworker, Katieka Bonner, was no longer working for CPS. Another caseworker had come and gone who never met us in person. That explained why there had been no contact and no monthly visit in July, and why I still didn't have formal Placement Papers. A little while later, the supervisor called Rufina back to ask the name of the Cypress Fairbanks Medical Clinic. She had not been able to find a phone number. Rufina explained, as patiently as possible, that it was Cypress Fairbanks Medical "Center," not "clinic" and looked up the number for her.

In spite of everything, we managed to leave, permission papers in my purse, on our trip to Tennessee. James was understandably restless on the two-day drive. It's funny how quickly one forgets what it's like to travel with young children. When our girls were young, we only managed a lengthy car trip to visit both sets of grandparents every other summer.

Our two grandchildren, each one an "only" child, are accustomed to being "center stage." It was amusing to watch how they handled competition with each other. Every time I had to do anything with James, even change a diaper or give him a bath, my granddaughter wanted to be right there in the middle of it. When I tried to sit down with my five-year-old granddaughter to read her a story, James somehow wormed his way between us. But we laughed, talked and enjoyed each other's company. We drove the "Cade's Cove" loop through Smokey Mountain National Park, went to the aquarium in Gatlinburg, and visited other tourist spots. The crowds of tourists put a bit of a damper on my enjoyment of the place. Loud laughter from rooms above and below us in the resort hotel and the drone of air conditioning units drowned out the songs of birds and the buzz of cicadas. It made me long for the quiet of our private place in Michigan's Upper Peninsula and also made me feel resentful once again that we could not go there.

Our daughter and son-in-law had to return home Sunday for their work week, so we spent that night by ourselves with James before heading back to Houston. James decided to have a temper tantrum at the TGI Friday's where we were trying to have dinner. We chose not to give him what he wanted, which was to run around outside, and tried to outlast his yelling while not allowing him to disturb other families around us. When one family gave us a long look, we pointed to him and said, "Sorry, he's two."

The father of three boys pointed to his crew, smiled and said, "Ten, eight and six. Would you like to trade?" We all laughed.

A young couple at the table across from us said they were celebrating their anniversary while their children's grandparents babysat. They began to worry whether their children were behaving.

When James saw he could not get what he wanted, he quit crying and ate his chicken strips and fries. His behavior on the way home was much better than on the drive to Tennessee.

The break from Houston had been good, but it was not a real vacation. Robbed of our summer to "recharge" before facing a new school year, we began August more exhausted than we had been in May. I used James's three days of day care the first week of August to sort out and organize all the materials in my classroom I had thrown into the closet so hastily in May.

Deborah K. Frontiera

I called the caseworker to let her know the name of James's daycare and tell her that I would be back at work full time beginning August 13, following my requirement to inform them of any change. When my message was finally answered, I was told our case had been "transferred" to a different unit. Elizabeth Bright was now our caseworker and Elizabeth Cantu the supervisor, bringing the number of CPS personnel involved with our case to nine. Ms. Cantu also told me that having the daycare fees paid did not depend on our level of income. We were eligible for that even if we made over "300% of poverty." She would start the paperwork, but it would "take a few weeks."

Ms. Bright came for her first home visit on August 20, arriving after I returned from my day of in-service. I had explained that I needed to be more careful of my use of personal leave. I didn't have unlimited days left after using up seven weeks worth the previous spring. I would need to participate in as many visits and appointments outside of school time as possible so I could use personal leave remaining for days when James or I were sick. Ms. Bright said she could certainly understand that. She also said she had not actually been given our case file. I spent a lot of time filling her in on background. She confided to me that this was her first job out of college and she was getting married the following week. I sighed; another caseworker younger than my daughter and with no experience would be controlling our lives.

I stated that I still had not received formal Placement Papers, gave her the address and phone number of the daycare center, and made sure she had all our work and cell phone numbers. I gave her yet another list of all the doctors involved and their phone numbers, explaining about CPS's responsibility to set up an Interdisciplinary Committee. I also asked her to find out the results of Rufina and Julio's psychological evaluations. They had been told to wait about three weeks to call for the results. Then they had been told that they would have to get the results from their caseworker, or make another two-hour-during-the-work-day appointment to get their own results. They could not afford any more time off, so they had waited to hear from a caseworker. Ms. Bright, of course, didn't know anything about any of it, since no one had given her the case file, but she promised to "check on" everything and call us.

Rufina and Julio were about half way through the parenting classes at that point. She described them as being little more than high school health and said she had learned more from reading *Parents Magazine* than the material given out in class. Other parents in the class had even more complaints about CPS and its caseworkers than we had.

One woman whose child was with a foster family said that every time she went to the CPS office for visits with her child, the caseworker would show up an hour or more late, cutting short her time to "continue to bond" with her child. She had two-hour visits every other week, so when the caseworker showed up late, her time with her child was cut to one hour or less. The caseworker was not faulted for such tardiness, but if the mother had shown up late, that would have been noted as a "lack of responsibility" on her part, furthering CPS' case for severing parental rights. Other parents complained of the same frustrations of caseworker changes, lateness, messages not returned, etc. that we had experienced.

It was good, in an ironic way, to find we weren't alone in our struggle. But it made us angry all over again about the whole situation. We were doing our part, but CPS was not doing its part.

I had a few email conversations with my sister who was a legal secretary at the time. She urged us to start our own "counter suit" against CPS, but later when she had a chance to talk to one of the attorneys at her firm about our case, the advice was that it would be extremely difficult to file any suit against a government agency.

The start of the new school year with its accompanying pressures added to our stress. My husband was easily agitated the first few weeks of any new school year. We began to pick at each other over little things as silly as who ate up some bit of left-over dinner. When big things are bothering you, little sparks light big fires. Reminders to back off or lighten up sometimes resulted in angry outbursts. The frustration of feeling you can't control your own destiny can get to you. I made the additional mistake of thinking I could manage to go with James, Rufina, Julio and his mother to the Children's Museum one Saturday morning and still make it home by noon to go with my husband and some friends to an afternoon movie. James was having a wonderful time at the museum; we forgot the time; then we stopped to have lunch, which also took longer that I expected. My husband had to call our friends and cancel. He was angry and I couldn't blame him.

Sometimes it took periods of not speaking to each other at all to cool off enough to talk in a way that we got at the root of the problem. Jasper felt like I always took "Rufina's side," didn't consider his feelings, and always did what they wanted. I couldn't deny that. He also felt he could not work quietly and uninterrupted on lesson plans or grade papers in the living room when Rufina and Julio were there in the evening with James. We discussed it with them and decided that they would skip visiting on Monday, Tuesday and Thursday evenings. This upset Rufina and Julio, but they had to agree. It had also become difficult for them to get "normal" housework done since they were spending so much time at our house. As much as it hurt not to see James some evenings, they agreed to the new schedule.

———— ◦•◦•◦ ————

August 23, I received a letter from CPS about another Permanency Planning Team Meeting. I called and said, "Didn't we have this meeting last May?"

"This is a five-month review for progress," the receptionist said.

I called Ms. Bright to confirm the date (September 11) and reminded her about the Placement Papers.

I had asked at different times whether Rufina might be allowed to take James to medical appointments "unsupervised" and had been told that was not possible. CPS always said they could have a caseworker take him if I couldn't go. I knew he would never go anywhere with someone who was, to him, a stranger. Ms. Bright, in her inexperience, could not understand this. There would be no exception. Either I took him or a caseworker would. Rufina absolutely could not take him anywhere unsupervised. Did they think she would run off with him? Or that she would do something foolish in a place as public as a doctor's office, which to me seemed quite supervised? It didn't matter. She couldn't take him unsupervised and that was that.

The reason I had asked was because James had another visit to the neurologist scheduled for August 28, the second day of school for students. In all my years of teaching, I had always avoided taking a day off during the first month to six weeks of school. Very young children have a hard enough time getting used to new routines and strange people when they start school. For many, it's the first time they have been away from their parents for any length of time during the day. They are insecure at best and crying with fright at worst. They need to see the same teacher every day until they feel secure. Under normal conditions, I would have to be unconscious in an emergency room to be absent from school during the first month. But we were not living under normal conditions. I secured the very best substitute teacher I could find for that second day of school, and the same person for all the upcoming meeting dates and court hearings that I knew of in advance. The four-year-olds in my class would just have to deal with it.

Fate threw me another curve ball. Federal regulations for Special Education had changed. Children could no longer stay in the Pre-school Program for Children with Disabilities (PPCD) if they were "speech only." In the past, the need for speech/language therapy had covered many children in whom teachers could see a need for special services but who might be too young for a specific diagnosis. Getting them into **some** program gave professionals a chance to find out what the specific needs were. Under the new regulations, children who had been in PPCD with a "speech only" label were required to go into regular pre-k classes whether they were ready or not. I would have three such children in my class (two of whom would later be diagnosed as Autistic). I also had a child who had Attention Deficit Disorder but was not on any medication because the ones that had been tried gave the child bad side effects. Two others were also probably hyperactive. Two more would be diagnosed later with developmental or emotional problems. Four were ESL (English as Second Language) and so low in their skills that I had to physically sit down when I said, "Sit down," for them to understand what I meant. So I had twelve children who needed a lot of special attention and ten other "normal" kids for a total of twenty-two four-year-olds.

Houston Independent School District does not assign a teacher's aid to pre-k classrooms. State law requires daycare centers to maintain an eleven-to-one ratio of children to adults with three and four year olds, but public schools, under the educational code, do not have that same requirement. Most school districts in Texas assign an aid at least part time in pre-k classrooms even though state law does not require it. Houston ISD follows all state laws "to the letter," and if they don't have to do something, they don't. I had all twenty-two children by myself.

The first day of school, half of them were crying when they came into the room. The others simply ran around getting into everything because they didn't know what they were supposed to do and apparently thought it was a great place to play. One parent took pity on me and stayed to help me get them settled down together on the carpet for the traditional "circle time." Three of them had tantrums after the parent left. I felt like I needed the arms of an octopus to get them to lunch. Fortunately, they all went to sleep at nap time so that I could put away their supplies and figure out how I would get them all to their various day care busses, car pool places, or to the hands of their parents at the end of the day. This was the group I would have to leave with a substitute the following morning because CPS wouldn't let my daughter take her child to a doctor appointment "unsupervised."

I drove to James's daycare after school thinking how nice it would be to put my feet up and let Rufina take care of James when she got off work. Then I remembered our new arrangement; it was Monday and I would be on my own, trying to play with James in his room until bath and bed time so we wouldn't bother Jasper. I wanted to cry.

———◆◆◆———

CHAPTER SIX

Living in Survival Mode

September 2, 2007, we celebrated our oldest daughter's thirty-fifth birthday. I have always taken time to think back to what I was doing at the same age each year when we celebrated her birthday. How different our lives have been. When I turned thirty-five, I had four children who were fourteen, ten, eight, and five years old. I was in the second year of my teaching career. Now, my oldest daughter was thirty-five, a single, professional CPA working as a consultant in internal auditing in the business world and earning more than her father and I combined. She owns her own home. I also thought about what my mother had been doing when she was thirty-five. I would have been five, and my siblings were six, nine, eleven and thirteen at the time. My mother was a typical 1950s housewife. Some people view the changes in women's lives over these generations as positive; others feel we should "go back" to those days of the 1950s. Change comes whether we like it or not, whether we think it's good or not. We cannot change the past and we can only hope to influence the future. All we have, on any given day, is the day itself and the reality of the moment.

We were all pretending to be happy on our oldest daughter's birthday in 2007. We did all the usual birthday stuff, but each of us had our own pain. Mary wished she could do more to help her sister through this difficult time. Rufina swallowed buckets of tears because she and her husband were caught up in CPS's chaotic "control" of their lives. My husband felt helpless, and therefore, frustrated and angry because he couldn't "fix" this mess like he could a stopped up drain or a computer that had frozen up and needed to have all its systems reinstalled. But we all loved each other and we were determined to survive.

We all craved stability and didn't have it. We wanted to get back to "normal" while knowing we could only try to figure out a new version of "normal." We kept up our smiles and soaked up each other's love like the angel food cake I had made soaked up the juice from the strawberries we poured over it.

—•◦••◦•—

My teaching job presented an entirely different form of "survival mode." Parents who seemed eager to volunteer at first were suddenly "busy." I couldn't blame them. I wouldn't have wanted to volunteer in my classroom either. I coped with multiple temper tantrums each day from three different students. I often used my cell phone to call the front office for help. (I had decided that using the school intercom system would not be a good idea. Using it would broadcast the tantrum noise all over the front office to be heard by any visitor who happened to enter the building at that time not a good first impression to leave with a visitor.) The clerk who answered the phone often said, "I'm sorry, Mrs. Frontiera, there's nobody here to send out there right now."

The only thing I could do was to carry the child having the tantrum to the corner and stand in front of him or her. That kept the child from being able to hurt others in the room or hurt him/herself. If the child pounded on my back in anger, I was so close that there was not sufficient force to hurt me. Then I was left with trying to direct the class from that vantage point. I would ask one of my few well-behaved children to pass out some drawing paper while I directed another to get out the crayons, hoping that coloring would occupy the rest of the class long enough to calm down the disruptive child. My days at school consisted of trying to maintain control, keeping children from getting hurt, and begging for help. No actual teaching was taking place.

I spent a couple of hours on the phone one evening with one of the lawyers at my professional organization trying to see what recourse I had, only to find out that the situation, sadly, was completely within Texas law. One form of recourse was to file a formal grievance, and I had to have a huge amount of formal documentation of asking for and being refused help to follow up on that option. My other choice was to invoke the state law which stated I could "put a child out of my classroom" for "severe disruption," and refuse to take the child back. That also required several weeks of formal documentation, steps of meeting with the parents of each child, calling a meeting of the school's Intervention Assistance Team, spending more weeks trying the recommendations of that team meeting . . . I met with my principal one day after school, begging again for an aid, to be told, again, that there were no funds to hire one and she had to take care of the kindergarten teachers first because they each had twenty-seven or twenty-eight kids. "In other words, I'd better not hold my breath," I said and walked out of her office biting my tongue to keep from screaming.

In the months of September and October, I filed four claims to Workman's Compensation for being bit, kicked, or scratched by tantrum throwers and having my knee cap dislocate when I tried to get up from sitting on the floor. (I had sat down next to one of my problem students to place a hand gently on his shoulder because I sensed a tantrum coming on. I was successful in keeping him calm, but my knee was not so fortunate when I tried to stand up.) Through all that, not once was one of the children hurt by a child having a tantrum I took that abuse. Rarely was anyone in the front office available to help. My notebook full of documentation began to grow thicker.

—•◦•◦•—

September 11 we were supposed to have another Permanency Planning Team meeting with CPS, the "five month review of progress." I had arranged for a substitute. Rufina and Julio had arranged for time off from their jobs. Their lawyer arrived on time. The mediator arrived to chair the meeting. Our caseworker was not there. We waited and waited. Finally, someone in that branch office of CPS called our branch office to see who was supposed to attend. Both our caseworker and her supervisor were in court all day. The previous caseworker had failed to inform the new worker and supervisor of the meeting, which had been set up months before that. They finally admitted that our entire file had been "misplaced." Another day of personal leave wasted.

I was livid. Rufina and Julio fought for control of their emotions because they feared having an outburst "in public" and how that would read into their record. This time even their lawyer was angry. He showed great control with a polite but firm complaint about all the things that had gone wrong with our case. The secretary at that branch office made polite apologies that I felt were insincere. The mediator let it be known he didn't appreciate it either.

Since I was already "off for the day," I went to our health club (something I had not done in a long time). A lengthy swim took the edge off my anger. I called the caseworker's supervisor's number, knowing I'd get voice mail, and with as calm a voice as I could manage, let her know that their failure to show up for the meeting was inexcusable and that I could not continue to take personal leave days "for nothing," because if I kept using leave that way, and I, or James got sick, it was possible that I might end up on "unpaid leave" and we could not afford that.

She actually called me back and apologized—the only apology I ever got from anyone at CPS. She told me that she could arrange for the rescheduled PPT meeting to be held during my conference period at school so I could attend by phone.

My arsenal of weapons for survival consisted of: visiting my chiropractor regularly, taking B vitamin supplements to support my adrenal system and fight stress, an occasional sleeping pill, and daily prayer as I drove to school. Sometimes I let tears pour out along with the prayer.

On September 21, I attended an early childhood conference sponsored by the Diocese of Houston/Galveston. I had been asked to do a workshop there on developing children's creativity through storytelling, but was able to take in other workshops when I had finished conducting mine. One that I attended covered spiritual aspects of stress and that loving the young children we chose to work with was a daily choice. The speaker's message was a much needed booster shot.

On the way home (driving my less-than-one-year-old vehicle) I saw two men in a rusted-out truck with the front bumper missing and a large crack in the windshield. A homeless man stood at another intersection hoping for handouts from people as they sat through a red light. We had also learned that a friend of our oldest daughter had been diagnosed with cancer. The following week, I learned that the mother of one of my students had finally gotten the courage to leave her bi-polar husband who would not stay on his medication and was threatening harm to all of them. She and her children were living in their car. After referring her to a couple of agencies for help, I said a prayer of thanksgiving for my blessings and prayed that I might change my attitude.

The rescheduled PPT meeting with CPS took place on time and I participated by cell phone during my forty-five minute planning period. I didn't think much had been accomplished, but my daughter told me later she had sensed a change in CPS's mood toward our case. In her email to family and friends she said:

> "We finally have a CPS team that is actually working (despite last month's delay). They finally have our Psych. Eval. Reports

and of course it recommended individual counseling (which our lawyer thinks everyone that goes in to have psych. evaluations gets whether they need it or not). We worked on suggestions of how to get the medical records (CPS blames the medical profession for this delay) for the Interdisciplinary Team gathered ASAP so the truth can come out and no further resources need to be wasted. The mediator suggested getting CPS lawyers involved to get the records, and we will go at them from our side. . . CPS did admit the delays in this case are their fault, and the mediator is planning on turning in a report stating that the delays are too long and there is no excuse for them."

(Quoted from the actual email with Rufina Bonilla's permission.)

My principal finally held Admission/Review/Dismissal meetings on my two autistic students who had been in the Preschool Program for Children with Disabilities the previous year for "speech only." Neither parent was prepared to accept the need for a different educational setting. Both parents clung to the hope, or misplaced belief, that their children would somehow "outgrow" their difficulties. It must be difficult for a parent of a special needs child to come to grips with a child's disability, but it has always seemed strange to me how some parents so staunchly refuse help for their children because they remain in denial of the problem. Rufina and Julio had accepted that James had special needs. Would CPS consider the parents of those children in my class "neglectful" because they denied that their children had problems?

We were back in court October 29, 2007, for another "progress" hearing. Our caseworker was actually early! She reported to the court that Rufina and Julio had completed their parenting classes, but that the counseling agency which had done their psychological evaluation wanted them to go to counseling sessions.

During the PPT meeting, thinking that they had completed everything, the thought that they still had to go to counseling nearly brought Rufina to tears. The caseworker explained to the judge (since Rufina and Julio's lawyer made an objection) that because we had been reassigned to so many different caseworkers, the results of the psychological evaluation had been delayed as they were passed from one worker to another. That was their official excuse. Rufina had called each caseworker more than once asking about the results, but all she had gotten was the usual, "I'll check into that."

Mr. Santulli, our lawyer, asked the caseworker during the hearing if she had received any of the medical records for the Interdisciplinary Team (which still had not taken place). When she said she had received some of them, he asked if she had read them and found any evidence of abuse. The county attorney for CPS objected to the question, but the judge overruled her objection. The caseworker answered cautiously, covering herself well, that she did not feel knowledgeable enough in such matters to say anything one way or the other. This was what Mr. Santulli expected her to say, but by asking, he got it into the court record that there was a medical possibility for James's original injury and that CPS had been wrong about our case from the start.

Still, the judge granted CPS their request to continue the case (in effect rubber-stamping their continued control over all our lives—better to err on the side of caution most judges would say) and set another court date for January of 2008. As the judge was giving Rufina and Julio his usual "reading of the rules," her eyes lowered as her heart sank with the repetition of each rule, despair creeping in with yet another delay. The judge noticed that her eyes were not on him and instructed her to look at him. She looked up immediately, unaware that anyone had noticed where her eyes were. From that point on, she made a conscious effort to keep it from happening again.

But we did win a small victory. Our lawyer made a request for "unsupervised" contact for transportation purposes. I had managed to explain to the lawyer some of our complicated schedules, especially on the days when I visited my chiropractor very late in the day after school faculty meetings. It was hard to get through with the chiropractic treatment on my neck and still get to James's daycare to pick him up before they closed. My husband had meetings on Wednesdays, too. Neither CPS nor the lawyer *ad litem* had any objections to Rufina picking James up from the daycare center and driving him five minutes to our house where either my husband or I would arrive within a few minutes. The judge's new order stated, "Limited unsupervised contact with a parent and the child is permitted for transportation purposes only."

He had not limited the order to trips between the daycare and home! This meant that Rufina could pick him up any day from daycare. I could come home from school and at least put my feet up for an hour or so of quiet on days I didn't have chiropractic therapy or meetings. It also meant that Rufina and Julio could transport him back to our house from church on Sundays. The Sunday following that court date they "transported" him around all day on a "detour" that lasted until supper time, giving my husband and me a much needed break. Houston's traffic congestion and the on-going construction on I-10 would give us unlimited excuses for "delays in transportation." Whether the judge had begun to see through CPS's mismanagement of our case and intended that or not, we will never know. But we were grateful for that broadly-worded order and certainly took advantage of it.

November 1, 2007, I picked up a certified letter from the post office containing the formal Placement Papers I had sought for so long. For over six months, we had cared for our grandson without this legal document from CPS. The papers were dated June 20, 2007. Apparently, the "misplaced" case file had finally been located.

Walker Counseling called Rufina on October 29, 2007, to set up an appointment for her and Julio. At their intake appointment, the counselor told them they would receive individual counseling but at the first appointment they would be together. That appointment took place on November 10, 2007. They were told their psychological evaluations looked "normal."

"Then why are we here?" Rufina asked.

There had been some "concern" over one of Rufina's answers on the psychological evaluation questionnaire. At the time, they had been told there were no "right or wrong" answers. One item had asked whether or not a "good spanking" hurt anyone. (Many recent scientific studies that followed families for over twenty years from the 1970s into the 1990s showed that the "couple of whacks on the rear" used by millions of families across the United States for generations, showed that there were no ill effects from this sort of "sub-abusive" discipline.) Rufina knew better than to reply "agree" with that item, but since "good spanking" was not defined as to whether it referred to a couple of swats on the rear or a beating that left marks, she had put "undecided" for that item. This, apparently, was the "concern."

Since CPS arranges and pays for parent counseling of this nature, and the results of that counseling determine whether or not children are to be returned to parents, I wondered whether **anybody** would be completely truthful in such sessions. The sessions could never be truly "confidential" since CPS would be looking over the report from the counselor. It would seem likely that most parents would be guarded, at best, in anything they said, and, at worst, downright deceptive, saying whatever they thought the counselor wanted to hear. (Rather like a person in prison putting on the best front for the parole board.) It would not be true counseling over real issues when it was forced upon a set of parents and they were not at liberty to choose their own counselor, one in whom they could trust and bare their souls. In addition to this was the fact that Walker Counseling dealt almost exclusively with CPS referrals. Their income came from the state. If they said a parent didn't need counseling, they received no money, so, of course, their inclination would be to recommend counseling for everyone and anyone sent to them by CPS.

———◆◆◆———

A person's immune system normally attacks and overcomes most viruses and infections floating around in the air. But constant stress keeps the immune system so busy coping with day-to-day life that it leaves one's body vulnerable to infections. Viruses and bacteria a-plenty floated around my pre-k class on a daily basis. I can't begin to count the number of times in a given year a parent sent a child to school with a note saying something like, "Little Joey was running a fever when he got up this morning, but he wanted to go to school, so I gave him some Tylenol and it went down." Sometimes, parents don't even send a note; they just drop off the sick child at school because they work for an employer who does not accommodate a parent who should stay at home with a sick child. When the choice is sending an ill child to school or losing a job, parents will choose the job so they can continue to provide for their children.

The sinus infection and laryngitis I came down with on November 10, 2007 hit so fast that by mid-afternoon I couldn't even whisper. Rufina arrived as soon as she got off work and took charge at our house. Sunday morning, since I couldn't even talk, let alone sing in choir, Jasper took James to church and left me at home. For the first time in months, I was alone in the house. I sat with my feet up on the couch drinking tea with honey and lemon. The only noises were the ticking of an antique clock I inherited from my mother, the whirr of the ceiling fan and the snuffling of our dog. The fan ruffled the curtains slightly, a movement I had not been able to notice amid the chaos of our lives. On Monday and Tuesday, I took James to his daycare and went home again to continue battling the sinus infection, which by then had moved into my ear.

The challenging children in my class gave my substitute problems while I was out and continued to make teaching extremely difficult when I returned. (The parents of the two autistic children still refused to allow placement in special education classes for their respective children.) While dealing with yet another temper tantrum, and hearing again from the clerk in the office that there was no one available to help, my knee cap slipped out of place again. Another round of Bio-freeze and another trip to the clinic that handled workman's compensation claims. This time, I was issued a knee brace and told to wear it every day at school.

———◦•◦•◦———

The following "conversation" took place by text message between Frank Santulli and Rufina on November 20:

> **Frank:** I have to subpoena records from CPS.
> **Rufina:** Why?
> **Frank:** So Ms. Bright won't get in trouble per her boss.
> **Rufina:** Get in trouble for what? Isn't it our right to see
> everything they have? Or is this just another delay tactic?
> **Frank:** I know. But they want me to formally request it.

(Quoted from Rufina Bonilla's phone record with her permission.)

The break at Thanksgiving gave our family some respite. Our daughter and son-in-law and granddaughter who lived in Tennessee came to spend the Sunday before Thanksgiving with us before going to our son-in-law's grandparents' home for Thanksgiving itself. Rufina's younger sister gave moral support through her presence. She seemed to sense that we were all tired of discussing the situation with CPS and never brought up the subject. We enjoyed the day together as a family and managed to pretend CPS did not exist. Rufina's sister had brought pictures from our trip in July, but Rufina found she could not look at them. The pictures were a reminder that her baby had taken a trip without her, not by choice as if he could travel with his grandparents because he wanted to, but because CPS had stated that she and James's daddy could **not** accompany us, even if they slept in a different motel room. Rufina held back her tears all day.

Someone, whose name I never did catch, from the Kinship Care Program finally came to our home to do a "home study" (paperwork to investigate us to make sure we would be suitable care-givers) on my husband and me on November 26, 2007, seven months after we had begun caring for our grandson.

The words of one of the Advent songs at church, "Patience, People, for the Lord is Coming," fit the mood of December. Patience, patience, and yet more of it was needed.

Walker Counseling presented the following "Treatment Plan" to Rufina and Julio at their December 1, 2007 appointment (Italics are mine):

> **Client(s) Name:** Julio Bonilla and Rufina Bonilla
> **County:** Harris
> **Therapist:** Denise Greenbaum
> **Case Worker:** Elizabeth Bright
> **Persons to be seen:** Julio Bonilla and Rufina Bonilla
> **Presenting Circumstances:**

Goals: 1. Increase parenting skills

2. Increase knowledge of son's medical diagnosis

3. Explore anger triggers and stress management

Progress Indications:

1. A. Mr. and Mrs. Bonilla reported that they completed parenting classes.

    B. Mr. and Mrs. Bonilla will develop a plan to meet their son's physical, developmental, and safety needs.

    C. Mr. and Mrs. Bonilla will explore interactions and dynamics in family of origin and identify values and traditions they plan to keep and one they plan to change.

    B. Explore Mr. and Mrs. Bonilla's philosophy of parenting and identify effective parenting strategies.

    C. Explore non-physical disciplinary techniques.

(Note the repetition in the outline A, B, C, B, C)

2. A. Mr. and Mrs. Bonilla will increase their knowledge of their son's medical diagnosis (seizure disorder) and treatment recommendations.

    B. Mr. and Mrs. Bonilla will consult with their son's physician.

3. A. Mr. and Mrs. Bonilla will explore anger and stress triggers.

    B. Mr. and Mrs. Bonilla will identify effective s strategies to cope with anger and stress.

Expected length of time: at least three months ____or closure of CPS case. (RB)

I, the client/guardian, agree to those objectives and I am aware that it is my responsibility to help achieve them. I understand that it is my therapist's responsibility to assist me in achieving these goals.

Signatures and the date December 1, 2007 were at the bottom of the page. The space after "Presenting Circumstances" was blank because the therapist had not received a copy of the original complaint from CPS. She was recommending counseling, but she didn't actually know why, except for what Rufina and Julio had told her. It brought to mind once again the presumption of guilt and the requirement that Rufina and Julio prove innocence beyond any doubt. In the list of counselor's recommendations, I noted that Rufina and Julio had been doing everything on that list long before CPS ever became involved. The following week, the counselor asked Rufina and Julio to supply a copy of the original complaint.

———•·•··•·•———

Another text message conversation between Rufina and Mr. Santulli took place after the December 1 session:

Rufina: Unless you can come up with a miracle, we have to go to counseling for the next 3 months.
Frank: When did you find this out?
Rufina: We just came from there and that's what the therapy sheet says unless the case is closed.
Frank: I'll come up with something. Will call.

———•·•··•·•———

When Frank received a faxed copy of the "Treatment Plan," his comment was that it looked like it addressed just about everybody in the world.

Frank went to the courthouse on December 12, 2007, to plead with the judge for unsupervised weekend visits, or at the very least, for Rufina and Julio to be able to spend Christmas Eve at our house so they could see James's reaction to Santa's filling of his stocking. The Court viewed James's case as a "blessing that he is with family" and other foster children needed attention more than he did. (I wondered whether if James had been in foster care, with the state paying the tab to the foster parents, CPS might have moved faster to resolve his case.) But The Court did grant permission for Rufina and Julio to spend the night of Christmas Eve at our house.

<hr />

It was also around the beginning of December when I went to my principal with an ultimatum of sorts. After my absence in November and the problems my substitute had had, she had actually asked me to be absent as little as possible! I told her I felt like I was falling apart physically and emotionally. I stated that I had to have help with my class. I mentioned that one of my options would be to file a formal grievance because if the conditions in my class didn't fit the description of "an intolerable work situation," I didn't know what did.

My principal offered a partial solution a few days later. I had often worked with the teacher of the three-year-old program for children with disabilities. About once a month for the previous two years, we had put our classes together for what we called "Friends Day." Those days were part of our attempt to include children with disabilities in activities with "normal" kids. I had always liked Friends Days because the special education teacher and I co-taught that day and we had her aid as well for yet another pair of hands to help. My principal now proposed that the special education teacher and I make every day "Friends Day." Since Ms. A only had two children in her morning group, we would co-teach every morning in my room from 8:30 until 10:30. This would give me the help needed during the "academic" portion of my day. The parent of the more difficult of my autistic children had finally agreed to allow her son to participate in one of the special education classes in the afternoon, so he would leave my group after lunch. Another tantrum-throwing child would be placed on half days with his daycare center picking him up after lunch. There would be two teachers and an aid with our combined twenty-four children in the morning, and in the afternoon, the two most difficult children would be gone. It was not a total solution, but it would be a big improvement.

———•◦••◦•———

I passed my sinus infection to Jasper (whose stress level was just as high as mine and immune system equally overworked) and he was as miserable, or more so, than I had been. He snapped at all of us for every little thing, even when the interruption was to offer him hot tea with lemon and honey. Putting up the Christmas tree was postponed until the very week before Christmas. Our large lighted Nativity figures for outdoors and the lights we usually put up along the roof line never made it out of the attic.

CPS hid behind the need to "follow procedures" and continued to lag in their responsibility to arrange the Interdisciplinary Team. Nothing was happening with them. Rufina and Julio reported that their counseling sessions seemed to be little more than fishing expeditions for a confession to their presumed guilt. They were asked to discuss things like, "With what you know now, what would you have done differently?" Rufina's response was that there was nothing they could have done differently. They had sought medical help with the first seizure and did everything their doctor told them to do. She was asked why she had not joined a support group.

She countered with the question, "When would I have time? I leave home at 6:30 AM for work and get home at 8 PM after putting

James to bed at my parents' house. And how would a support group help me with CPS?"

Julio's response to the question about what he would have done differently was that he would always be sure to get complete copies of every medical record and carry them around whenever going to a new or different doctor was required.

My sister, a legal secretary at a large firm in New York, called to say she had discussed our case again with one of the partners in her firm. (We were still toying with the idea of filing a counter suit against CPS for their incompetent handling of our case.) The partner's advice was not to bother filing any suit against a government agency. It would be extremely difficult to win such a case. CPS would simply stand behind a defense of "doing their jobs" and needing to check things out "just in case" and they would probably prevail. Government agencies would always set themselves up as infallible gods no matter what.

Patience, patience. Ours was running thin.

———◆◆◆———

CHAPTER SEVEN

Round and Round the Mull Berry Bush

Rufina spent the night at our house Christmas Eve, sleeping in her sister's bed in the room with James's crib. Her sister, home from college between semesters, once again occupied the other bedroom which had been my husband's "office." Julio came over early Christmas morning. We were happy but not happy. Smiles were forced, and I didn't write about the day in my journal.

New Year's Eve passed like any other night. We didn't even stay awake until midnight. I began 2008 with depressing thoughts about "Time" as an arbitrary measure. Cynicism moved into my heart and brain. I made no resolutions so I would have none to break, hence no disappointments. The only thing I felt positive about was the knowledge that in June of 2008 I would be eligible to retire from public school teaching in Texas. Ninety-five student attendance days remained before the school year ended—fewer than one hundred I could survive.

January also brought out my principal's ulterior motive for my partnership with the special education teacher. While part of her goal was to get me enough help to prevent me from filing a formal grievance, she also played the public relations' ace by inviting some district supervisors in to observe how well our partnership was going and how "all the children were benefiting." Ms. A and I (good friends as well as colleagues) rolled our eyes at each other but said nothing.

January doldrums set in as they never had before. Lack of daylight. No Christmas lights on houses to make up for the long, dark nights. Cloudy days blended into darkness. But neither Jasper nor I slept well. Rufina and Julio were not sleeping well either. The empty bedroom down the hall haunted them and they were still unable to open the door.

One day part of a song popped into my head about the passage of time:

> "While summer-salting at a cockeyed angle
> It (Earth) makes a cockeyed circle round the sun
> And when . . . something, something I couldn't remember
> It gets back where it started from
> Another year is done.
> And there's no way to stop it, no there's no way to stop it
> No, you can't even stop it if you try.
> So I'm not going to worry and I'm not going to hurry
> Every time I see another year go by."

(Quoted from memory and used under the provisions of Fair Use.)

At that point in the song, my mind would go blank and I would be unable to remember the rest of the words. Later, with the help of a niece who teaches music, I learned that the song was from an early stage production on *The Sound of Music* that had been left out of the movie version. I had seen that stage version as a child, long before the movie. Now, even the movie was old. Why would that song pop into my head after all those years? Whatever the reason, the silly song cheered me a bit and I let it keep running through my head humming through the parts where I could not remember the words.

Rufina and Julio found comfort in a country western song by Rodney Atkins that was on the radio a lot around that time: "If you're going through Hell, keep on going. Don't slow down; if you're scared, don't show it. You might get out before the Devil knows you're there."

Rufina and Julio had another counseling session January 5, 2008. This session focused on the concept of "good" or "bad" spankings, the question on the psychological survey to which Rufina had stated "undecided." In her session, Rufina defined an "okay" spanking as two or three swats on the bottom that didn't leave a mark. In Julio's portion of the session, he focused on the fact that things were different now-a-days and it was no longer like it was when he was a kid. He brought up changes in schools and some of his experiences at his current job as a school bus driver. The counselor seemed satisfied with their answers but asked Julio to fill out the original survey again. He had apparently "not passed" a "test" in which there were supposed to be "no wrong answers."

Their last session took place January 19, 2008. This session seemed to be yet another fishing expedition. The counselor told Rufina a story about someone she knew who had been abused as a child and then she abused her own child and acted like that was normal because it was what she had grown up with. Rufina stared at her with a puzzled look and asked herself, *Where is she going with this?* She asked the counselor what she meant.

The counselor rephrased by saying, "If you were abused as a child and now you were ignoring that fact that your child was abused because you saw it as normal."

Okay, Rufina thought, *now I know where she's going.* She answered, "I still don't know what you are talking about. I was never abused as a child. I grew up in a normal home."

At that, the counselor ended her session and began Julio's session. At the end of both sessions, the counselor told them she would send her report to their caseworker and they needed to wait to hear if more sessions were required. CPS neither replied to Walker Counseling's report (that we were informed about), nor informed Julio and Rufina whether they had been released. Their lawyer told them at that point, it was better for their case to stop calling CPS entirely and make notes about the lack of contact from them.

During these same weeks, I received a letter from the University of North Texas asking me to participate in a survey concerning the Texas Health and Services Commission. They were contacting people who had received services from Child Protective Services and the Kinship Program. I filled out the survey giving CPS the lowest possible ratings and providing contact information in case anyone wanted more details. I was not contacted again.

That same weekend, Jasper and I made the decision to let Rufina stay at our house while we **both** went to the wedding reception of a friend's daughter who lived in another part of Texas. We needed a joyful break. The heck with what the court said about unsupervised over-night visits! If CPS didn't take the time to do the regular, monthly visits they were **supposed** to do, the chances were almost zero that they would drop by unannounced (as they had the right to do) on a weekend. We decided that "right" to make "unannounced" visits was a lot of fear-mongering they used to keep people in line. Such Gestapo tactics would no longer work on us. We left telling Rufina all she had to do was **not** to answer the door unless somebody produced a warrant. No one dropped in.

We had a lovely time at the reception but left early because we were both tired. Alone in a motel for the first time in months, we were both asleep by 8:30 PM and didn't wake until past 7 AM. It was the best sleep we had had in a long time. Besides longing for more "aloneness," we decided perhaps it was time for a new mattress. We stopped to look at, and purchased for immediate delivery, a mattress at a good store in Houston before reaching home that Sunday.

A school year in Houston ISD has 175 student attendance days. The day after Martin Luther King Day marked the half way point of the school year. At noon on the eighty-seventh day of the school year, I announced to Ms. A that there were now fewer days remaining than I had already survived. She laughed and gave me a hug. Many people do not realize that teachers of young children usually count the days of school and celebrate the 100th day. The count of days provides many learning experiences about number, counting, place value, and perhaps a dozen other math concepts in the state-mandated curriculum. For me, especially that year, subtracting the number of days gone by from 175 gave me an instant knowledge of how many days remained. My joy at passing the half-way point that year was a pathetic reminder of how burned-out I had become.

•◦•◦•

January 28, 2008, I answered the phone to be told by a caseworker named Lashala Taylor, "I just got this case today." This was our tenth different caseworker. She wanted to set up a time for a home visit, our first since October. We would meet with her on January 31. James had an appointment with his regular neurologist that morning, so I would already be off from school. (Rufina always came to James's doctor appointments but would have to return to work after we left the doctor. January starts tax season and the clients at her firm needed their CPA.) By 5:10 PM on the January 31, Lashala had neither called nor shown up for our 3:15 appointment.

James had another appointment with the neurosurgeon on February 4. (My class had yet another day with a substitute, and would again the following Monday when I had my own physical to contend with, but at least I had managed to schedule my eye doctor appointment for the afternoon on that same day.) The neurosurgeon, as had the neurologist the week before, said James was doing very well, gradually "growing into the size of his head." His balance had improved and, while his helmet was still recommended for outdoor play at his daycare center, he would not need it otherwise.

Our world seemed a bit brighter as Lent began two days later, and I determined to work at regaining a more positive focus on life. The following Monday, my doctor declared that I was in generally good health. We discussed the stressors in my life, but since much of the stress was beyond my ability to control, there was not much more I could do about it than I was already doing. Then our other married daughter called to say she had had a miscarriage. She had been so excited when she'd called a few weeks earlier to announce her pregnancy, and I'd been happy to think the birth would happen after I had retired and would be able to go to her and help out. Now, I couldn't go to her, couldn't even help her through the "emotional down" except by phone.

———————

Ms. Lashala Taylor called on February 14 to reschedule the home visit. I asked what had happened to the last one. She had had the flu, she stated, and her supervisor was supposed to call.

"Well, nobody called," I said.

"I'm sorry about that," she replied.

Both our schedules were pretty full, but we managed to set a time of 5:30 PM on February 19, less than a week before our next court date.

It was another routine first visit. She arrived late, but at least used a cell phone this time to call and inform us. The same old questions were asked the same old way that we had answered countless times before. The same comment about the adult bed in his room and the same response that no one slept in there regularly; there was no place else to put the bed. The same response when I said that we had been promised funding for daycare and had not received anything: I'll check into it. And: no she hadn't read the file because she hadn't received it yet.

When I asked who would be testifying in court, the response was that her supervisor would be. *Great*, I thought, *another person who won't know what's going on.*

⸻ ⚬•⊷•⚬ ⸻

Mr. Santulli reassured us that everyone (CPS's lawyer, the lawyer *ad litem* and himself) agreed that James would be returning home after court on February 25, 2008. Rufina and Julio kept telling us everything would be fine. I remained hopeful but doubtful. Jasper was downright skeptical, reminding us that every time we had gone to court, CPS had pulled some new stunt. In spite of that, Rufina and I packed up most of his things the evening before. James beamed when his mommy told him he would be going home the next day.

Even though I tried mightily to hold all the details in my mind that morning, some parts still blurred due to anger and frustration. We met the CPS supervisor, Marilyn Thomas, for the first time outside the court room. Ms. Thomas said she had read the file but wanted some more background before we went before the judge. She expressed surprise that things had dragged on so long and asked if I was receiving payments for daycare, etc.

"Not a dime," I said. "The only help we've gotten are the vouchers from WIC."

"I'm sorry, I'll check into that," she said. *Where have I heard that before?* I thought but said nothing.

The rest of her questions concerned James's medical records and family background—all the usual questions answered in the usual way.

We entered the court room. Our case was called and we approached the bench and were sworn in. The CPS lawyer proceeded first and questioned Ms. Thomas. Her responses, summed up to the best of all our memories stated that: she had only had the case a few days but there seemed to be the possibility that James's injuries were related to his seizures (as we had been saying for nearly a year). She wanted to have more time to have the Interdisciplinary Team meet (which the court had told them to do ten months earlier) and that she had not had time to do a "home study" on Rufina and Julio's home (indeed, no CPS worker had **ever** entered their home at that point) to be sure James would return to a "safe" environment.

Suddenly the CPS lawyer was asking Ms. Thomas if she was saying she needed a continuance of the case!

And the judge granted it!

Mr. Santulli managed to get in a deadline of March 14, 2008, for CPS to complete the home study (as if they had met any other deadlines) and then Judge Glick set a June 16, 2008, hearing date, banged his gavel and called the next case.

Clearly out of order, confused and angry, I spoke up, in as controlled a manner as possible. "Excuse me. I'm really confused. I came here today with the assurance that James would be going home today and now you are saying he's not?"

"That's correct," was the response, although I don't recall who said it. We were ushered out of the court room. Somewhere in there, the judge did thank me for continuing to care for James.

Outside the courtroom I nearly exploded but in a semi-controlled harsh, whisper said, "Would somebody please tell me what the *expletive* just happened here?"

Mr. Santulli moved us all over to a quiet corner.

Rufina was in tears and about to collapse. "What are we going to tell James now? We promised him he was coming home today." Julio put his arms around her, his eyes wet, too.

Mr. Santulli said that he had been just as surprised as we were by the turn of events and that, while Ms. Thomas seemed to have the best of intentions in asking for more time, she had opened a whole can of worms that hadn't needed to be opened.

After a few minutes to calm down, we returned to the conference room with Ms. Thomas. I handed her my copy of all of

James's medical records (which I always carried to court dates in a large plastic file folder) and she began to glance through them. She used her cell phone to contact a Dr. Sharp (PhD. not M.D.) and asked him if he could come to the courthouse immediately. She told us Dr. Sharp was a nurse consultant who worked for CPS. While we waited for him to arrive, Ms. Thomas asked me if she could **have** my copy of all the records, the copy that CPS had said back in May of 2007 was not what they needed because it didn't have the necessary legal language.

Remembering what I had gone through to obtain the records and how CPS had "misplaced" our entire file for several weeks, and that a caseworker had earlier stated that CPS **had** all his records, I said, "No. According to your previous caseworkers, you supposedly have all these records already. If you like, we can find a copy machine here in this building and I'll stand by while you make a copy, but this set is not leaving my sight."

Ms. Thomas said she would locate the CPS copies.

When Dr. Sharp arrived, he talked with Rufina and Julio in great detail. They related the entire saga to him, calmly and precisely. He (in a change of attitude for CPS) said he believed them, and that he would "get right on this," meaning he would get the Interdisciplinary Team together within the next two weeks. He also admitted that many parts of the CPS system were "broken" but that he wanted it to work for us in this case. He gave each of us one of his cards and said we could call or email anytime.

I managed to ask Ms. Thomas if it would be possible for Rufina to begin taking James to doctor and dental visits without me, explaining that I had a limited number of days of personal leave left and that I wanted to have enough days to be able to use "paid days" when our youngest daughter graduated from college in May. She said that she had no problem with that. I asked if we needed some sort of paper work for the doctor's office staff, since I was supposed to sign all forms. She stated clearly that we didn't need any paperwork.

We didn't leave the courthouse until nearly 11 AM. Rufina and Julio tried to look at the "bright side" saying that these steps would allow them to prove innocence and clear their names. Early on, the lawyer's advice had been to do everything CPS said, smile, play the game and it would "all go away" but they wanted their names cleared for the future.

I was still so angry with CPS for waiting all those months before finally doing any real investigation I thought I might slug someone. Crying and exercising at our health club (since I already had the day off and James was at daycare) did not get rid of my frustration completely. When I got home, I grabbed a half empty box of Girl Scout Thin Mints and didn't stop eating until the box was empty. Then I stared at the empty box, angry at myself for the binge, and cried again.

—•◦•—

My feelings were nothing compared to those of Rufina and Julio, and worse yet, James. Rufina went back to work. Her boss knew that they had been expecting to get James back and asked how it went. Rufina broke down and the tears would not stop. All her boss and co-workers could do was hug her, pat her back and tell her how sorry they were. The progress we had made in getting him to bed without fussing and crying evaporated. He didn't understand and there was no way to explain to a two-year-old what we, as adults, didn't understand. Children his age are at the tantrum stage as it is. Our circumstances were far beyond his ability to comprehend or control. We had to return to the practice of letting him cry himself to sleep. Except that now, he had learned to climb out of the crib. We couldn't close the door knowing he would be safe in the confines of his crib.

It often happened that Julio's hours at his job prevented him from coming over on weekday evenings. When he did come, James's crying upset him so much that he began to avoid coming even when he got off early enough.

Even though Ms. Thomas had said that we didn't need a letter for Rufina to take James to doctor and dentist appointments, several friends and my sister said that we **should** have a letter formally stating that CPS approved this type of "unsupervised visit." I called Ms. Thomas on February 26, 2008, and left a voice mail to that effect. She returned my call on February 27 and said that she had to be out of town for a few days but would take care of it as soon as she got back the following week. She did thank me for all the family was doing and continued to assure me that she would get the case wrapped up as soon as possible.

Rufina began to think more critically about the in-depth questioning the morning of the hearing. Was all of that merely another attempt to get some sort of "confession?" It seemed, as a result of their experiences in the parenting classes, that parents who admitted they had abused their children got custody back more quickly. But neither Rufina nor Julio were about to "confess" to something that never happened.

On February 29, 2008, our lawyer talked with the lawyer *ad litem* about going to the judge to modify visitation rules to include over-night visits. The lawyer *ad litem* advised Frank not to file such a motion. He related to our lawyer that while he didn't like the system, trying to hurry it along can "tick off the judge" and that would not be a good thing.

In a text message to Rufina, Frank relayed that both the judge and the lawyer *ad litem* expected the case to be over by March 14. In a return text, Rufina asked:

"If CPS doesn't do the home study by the 14th, will the judge hold them accountable?"

Frank: No.
Rufina: If CPS doesn't meet deadline, then will you file motion?
Frank: I'll see what I can do. Maybe call Austin again.

(Quoted from Rufina Bonilla's phone records and used with her permission.)

———•••———

By February 26, I had already emailed the Office of Consumer Affairs, outlining the problems with the way our case had been handled. I received a reply on February 27:

"Dear Ms. Frontiera:
Your concerns have been received by the Department of Family and Protective Services (DFPS) Office of Consumer Affairs (OCA). This information is being reviewed. In the meantime, should you have questions or additional information, please call Dr. Maryann Fisher in the OCA at 1-800-720-7777. Karen Monreal, Admin. Assistant, DFPS Office of Consumer Affairs."

(Quoted from the letter in the author's possession.)

I called February 28th and provided more information on the delays and other problems we had encountered. I didn't hear anything more from the OCA.

In between all of that, I lost another two days of personal leave to an ear infection that responded only to the newest, strongest, antibiotic on the market. My doctor had wanted me to rest at home a third day, but, unable to find a substitute willing to take my class (my usual substitutes were already booked) I had to stick it out at school.

I waited until Friday, March 7, to call Ms. Thomas again about the letter for doctor and dental visits. She was not in. I left a voice mail around 11:35 AM. My call was not returned before the end of that business day. I called again on Monday, March 10. She finally called me back on the March 12 to say she could not write me a letter concerning doctor and dental visits until **after** James's medical records had been checked by a forensic team. This directly contradicted what she had said after the hearing about her not having a problem with Rufina handling such appointments alone and not needing a letter in the first place!

She further contradicted herself by telling me that she would have all the medical records by that same day (Wednesday, March 12) and then telling me "tomorrow" (Thursday, March 13). Then she asked me if I remembered whether the judge had said to have the home study paper work **to** him by March 14, or simply completed by that day. My mind had been in such a fog as a result of the hearing that I gave her the benefit of the doubt and said I thought the deadline was to have the home study finished by CPS. This still only gave her two more days to complete it. I tried to be helpful by giving her Rufina and Julio's work schedules and phone numbers, which she didn't seem to have available, again. I made a bet with myself that she would not meet the deadline.

The day we had been at the hearing, Dr. Sharp, R.N. PhD. had told Rufina she could contact him any time. What follows is a series of emails they exchanged, quoted exactly as they were sent and received.

> **From:** Rufina Bonilla; Sent: Wed., Mar. 05, 2008, 12:00 PM,
> **To:** Tyrone Sharp; Subject: Medical Review
> **Tyrone,** I was just wondering what was happening with the medical review for James Bonilla. Thanks, Rufina Bonilla

> **From:** Sharp, Tyrone; Sent: Wed. Mar. 05, 2008, 4:51 PM
> **To:** Rufina Bonilla; Subject: Medical Review
> *(No message included)*

From: Rufina Bonilla; Sent: Thurs. Mar. 06, 2008, 7:44 AM
To: Sharp, Tyrone; Subject: Medical Review
Tyrone, Did you mean to send me a blank response? Thanks,
Rufina Bonilla

From: Sharp, Tyrone; Sent: Thurs. Mar. 06, 2008, 1:33 PM
To: Rufina Bonilla; Cc: Sharp, Tyrone; Subject: Medical Review
Thursday, March 6, 2008, 1:24 PM
Greetings Ms. Bonilla, I am sorry. I thought that I had typed in
a response. Can you find it in your heart to forgive me (please)?
We are awaiting receipt of the medical records. It is my
understanding that the records will be available for review at our
3 Northpoint office by Wednesday, March 12, 2008. When the
records are received I will forward them to the Forensic
Assessment Center for final review and outcome. So, please be
patient with me. I have not forgotten about our need to come to
closure ASAP. As well, call me as you determined necessary,
Regards, Tyrone Sharp, R.N. Ph. D, Region 6 Nurse
Consultant, 2525 Murworth Dr., Suite B2-45, Houston, TX
77054   (713-394-4008)

(Quoted from the actual emails and used with Rufina Bonilla's permission.)

Rufina decided to continue with emails rather than phone
calls, since printing them out documented the communication with
absolute accuracy, while notes on a phone call can become "hearsay"
and are easy to deny. Contradictions, such as those I was hearing on
the phone with Ms. Thomas, couldn't be denied when they showed
up in print. These emails would continue to accumulate over the
coming weeks.

Right on March 14, at the very end of the day, Ms. Thomas
(after getting lost twice) arrived at Rufina and Julio's home. I was

pleased to lose the bet with myself. She turned on the water in the kitchen sink and in both bathrooms and flushed the toilets. She flicked light switches on and off. She looked inside the refrigerator and pantry and looked in James's room. This was the first time they had been in his room since taking out the crib. It felt as they had feared—cold and empty.

Seeing no bed, she said, "I assume his bed is at your parents'."

"Yes," Rufina responded.

She noted that they had a hearth guard covering the sharp edge in the brick bench in front of their fireplace. She asked to see the photos taken when CPS had come earlier, so she could compare "before" and "after." This was supposedly to demonstrate that Rufina and Julio's home had been improved for safety as a result of CPS involvement.

When Rufina told her that there were no pictures because no one from CPS had **ever** visited their home, Ms. Thomas seemed surprised. She also seemed surprised when Rufina told her that it had taken less than one hour for the original decision to remove James from a home CPS had never seen.

Later that same evening, Ms. Thomas called me to ask if I had the films from the February 20, 2007, CT scan Cypress Fairbanks Medical Center. I said that I did not have them, that I had borrowed them to take to Texas Children's, and that I assumed Texas Children's had returned them, since I had been told they would. I also indicated (since the following week was spring break and I was off from school) that I would be willing to drive out there and borrow them again and deliver them by hand to Dr. Sharp if that would expedite the matter.

Ms. Thomas also asked me again when our kinship home study had been done and whether I was receiving payments for the daycare. (By this time, our family had paid nearly $4000 in daycare fees out of our pockets.) I told her we had not received any money.

All of us were feeling like hamsters running in an exercise wheel, faster and faster but getting nowhere.

Monday, March 17, 2008, I got off the nowhere-wheel briefly for an early brown bag lunch with a friend who works at a nature preserve. Sitting outside (while James ate a peanut butter sandwich) in the spring sunshine of natural forest for an almost uninterrupted visit was a brief moment of respite. Then I headed, James in tow, to Cypress Fairbanks Medical Center to borrow the films again, only to discover upon reaching the proper office that I had forgotten to take the Placement Papers showing that I had legal permission to pick the films up. I called my husband but he couldn't find them to fax to the hospital. I explained the situation and how long it would take me to drive home and drive out there again. The office receptionist talked to her supervisor, who, thankfully, had a good amount of common sense. They let me check out the films since I had James's Medicaid letter in my purse and it had our address, which matched the address on my driver's license. Dr. Sharp later came to my house and picked the films up from me.

Rufina received an email from Dr. Sharp on March 21 that the case was now "in review."

———◦•◦•◦———

CHAPTER EIGHT

Switching to Offense

S pring break ended with Easter that year, the earliest date for Easter (March 23) in 200 years due to the fact that a full moon appeared on Spring Equinox, which came on March 20, 2008.

The seating around our dining room table was completely full with family and a college friend and her daughter (a year younger than my oldest) visiting from Michigan. My friend had arrived on Friday to spend her spring break with her daughter who was working as a contract nurse in Galveston. We had taken them to Reliant Park on Saturday for a full day (the last day) of that year's Houston Rodeo. The fun of the rodeo (a totally new experience for our visitors) relieved the stress of the on-going CPS battle.

As a family, we also decided it was time to take back our lives. A month had gone by since the court date and we were no farther along in getting James home than we had been on the court date. We decided that if CPS took its usual turtle pace, we would probably have to wait until June to end things. We needed to make arrangements for travel in May to attend our youngest daughter's graduation from Pratt Institute in New York. Both Jasper and I wanted to be there. It would be more than three days "out of jurisdiction" and a college commencement ceremony is not something a two-year-old would be able to sit through, so we would have to make some other arrangement. All of that would take paperwork from CPS, which they never did in a timely fashion.

Rufina and Julio's friends who lived in Brenham told us they would be glad to take care of James for our trip to New York. Carlene and Rufina had been friends since grade school. Carlene's husband Mike was James's godfather. Their children and James had been together on weekends several times.

Rufina and Julio also decided that if things were not resolved by the end of the school year, Jasper and I should go ahead and take James with us to our summer place in Michigan's Upper Peninsula. While it would be hard on them to be away from him for two months, they felt we had done enough when we gave up the previous summer.

"Well, we could leave later in June, after the next court date," I said.

"No, go ahead and go when school is out. They never ask you anything during the hearings and James doesn't have to be there. If we finally get him back, we'll drive up and get him."

"Are you sure?"

"Yes."

"Well, I guess your dad will have his little fishing buddy a few years sooner than we thought."

Much later, Rufina told me that she had not been sure at all when she said, "Yes," but didn't feel there was any other choice at that time.

Within my own mind, I decided that I wasn't going to **ask** CPS if it was okay to do all this. I was simply going to **inform** them of our plans. When Ms. Thomas called on March 24 to tell me the daycare fees had been approved, I told her I needed travel forms for the May trip and gave her Carlene and Mike's address and telephone number. Ms. Thomas said a home study would have to be done to approve Carlene and Mike. I told her to get on it, because we **would** be going. I left a reminder message with her secretary on March 27. Instead of putting our lives on hold and waiting for CPS to do their part, we would assume that James would be with us indefinitely and go on with our lives, including James, but doing what we wanted to do.

The following weekend Rufina and Julio took James to Carlene and Mike's for the weekend. We were completely through fooling around with the scare tactics of possible unannounced visits. I traveled to Amarillo, Texas, for a writers' conference. (I had critiqued several manuscripts for the sponsoring organization's contest and was invited to attend for free.) Jasper got some quiet time for himself at our house.

March 31, 2007, I actually got Ms. Thomas on the phone. I asked her to get the ball rolling on a home study for Carlene and Mike. She told me that the forensic team "might" finish that week. She also asked for the address and phone number of James's daycare (something I had sent them in writing several times previously) because she wanted to visit the facility.

April 3, Rufina sent Dr. Sharp a message asking if there was any news. She did not receive a reply. She emailed Frank Santulli on April 8, stating:

> "My mom talked to Marilyn [Thomas] yesterday. Marilyn told her that the forensic assessment should only take two weeks. However, the reason for the delay in our case is that the previous caseworkers did not have all the records that they told us they did (which was probably the real reason why they told you that you needed a subpoena to get the records they had). Also, she said that they should have a decision by Wednesday (my response was 'of which week?'). My mom asked her if we would have to go to court once the decision came back, or would they just send James home. Marilyn said that she had the power to just send him home, but at some point we would need to go to court to close the case. We will still continue to email them to make sure we do not fall through the cracks again. Have you heard anything around the courts with the lawyers?"

Mr. Santulli replied by email the same day and stated:
"No . . . they have not contacted me in any way . . . Lynn
Chamberlin, DA, can't say much because they are her client . . .
but I can tell she things it's bs."

(Quoted from the actual email provided by Rufina Bonilla and used with her permission.)

——•••—

The following dialogue took place in emails between Rufina
and Dr. Tyrone Sharp on April 10:

11:40 AM, Rufina to Sharp: Tyrone, is there any news yet?
    Thanks, Rufina.

11:44 AM, Sharp to Rufina: Not at this time.

11:47 AM, Rufina to Sharp: The last couple of weeks you told
us that this was coming to a decision soon. How soon is soon?
    Thanks, Rufina

From: Sharp, Tyrone P.
Sent: Thursday, April 10, 2008, 12:07 PM
To: Rufina Bonilla
CC: Thomas, Marilyn J., Sharp, Tryone P
Subject; RE
Thursday, April 10, 2008, 11:56 PM CDLST
Ms.Bonilla,
A decision will be forthcoming. I have no control over when the
physicians actually complete and write the report. I assured your
mother, you, and your husband and your attorney that I would
walk everything through and I have done that. So, no need to
become impatient or to **become distressed at this juncture. We**

will get the report and the medical statements when they are read. Have a great day and a wonderful weekend! (*bold font his*)

Sincerely, Dr. Tyrone Parker Sharp, R.N.,

Region 6 Nurse Consultant, 2525 Murworth Dr.

Houston, TX 77054, (713) 394-4008 Office

(cell number followed)

12:14 PM Rufina to Sharp: It is not that I am impatient or distressed. It is just that we have been promised so many things in the past and then CPS goes back on what they say. We have done everything that CPS asked us to do, and yet, Sunday marks a year that we have been in this nightmare. We are just wondering when it will end.

2:02 PM (same headings as above) Sharp to Rufina: Greetings, Mrs. Bonilla, I appreciate your experience and I am glad to know that you are not impatient and that you are not distressed. So, it appears that we are all in a good place. In closing, when the reports and medical statements are ready then we will all be able to proceed in a manner that is appropriate. I will be in touch.

Dr. Sharp

(Quoted from emails provided by Rufina Bonilla and used with her permission.)

I received a call from Ms. Thomas on my cell phone (during my students' nap time at school) asking if I had ever received the $1000 stipend that the kinship program gives families providing care to children in CPS custody. I told her, again, I had not received any money. She said she would check on it. Later that afternoon, I received a message from a person in the kinship office. The voicemail was garbled, but the number was clear. I returned the call as soon as school was out. I was told that our income was "too high" and we did not qualify for anything but daycare. I asked if we would receive any "back pay" for all the daycare we had already incurred. I was told we would not. I asked how much, on average, the state paid to a foster family. She said it depended on the level of care but the average was $20 per day, or $400 per month.

The entire situation was much more than a matter of dollars and cents, but I sat down with a paper and pencil and did a little math. Calculating both ways by day or by month I figured that, from the previous April to that date, we had saved the State of Texas somewhere between $4800 and $7200 that they had not paid to a foster home for James's care, and had spent nearly $4000 on daycare for which we would never be repaid (not to mention thousands in legal fees). But, on two teaching salaries, we were "too rich" to be reimbursed a mere $1000 stipend to help with our expenses. Rufina and Julio provided all James's clothing and diapers. They paid most of the daycare until we finally won that battle. (A much more expensive daycare than they had had before.) They tried to help in other ways as well.

In my journal, I rambled at length about whether I was being selfish, or not, and wavered between guilt and anger. I struggled with the whole idea of "forgive and forget." I came to two conclusions: Jesus was not afraid (and certainly felt no guilt) when he criticized the pharoses of his day, so I should not feel afraid or guilty for speaking out about the injustices of CPS. Jesus vented his anger upon the money-changers in the temple, so my anger was not wrong. What was important was for me to direct my anger in a constructive way that might prevent the agony we were going through from happening to others.

A few days later, CPS forcibly took custody of over 400 children from a polygamist sect near San Angelo, Texas. While I do not believe in polygamy, or underage marriage, I empathized with the plight of those parents. CPS used the same "eminent danger" emergency removal that they had invoked in our case. I wondered what "eminent danger" those children had been in.

The morning of April 15, I had my car loaded to leave after school and drive to Dallas to attend the Texas Librarian Association State Conference with my picture book publisher. Rufina would pick up James from daycare, and I had lined up the best substitute teacher on my school's list for the three days I would be gone. I never got there.

Shortly before lunch time, I felt extremely dizzy. I leaned on the toy refrigerator in the playhouse center and tried to remain calm in front of my students. My co-teacher had left the room after recess, so I was alone. I managed to wobble to my chair in front of the group and sat down. A second wave of dizziness hit and I crumpled to the floor. I think it was only a few seconds, but the children were quite upset, asking if I was okay.

"I'm fine," I lied. "I'm just not feeling well. I think I'll sit while we sing and take turns in the restroom. Can you help me by doing the right things?"

They all nodded, even my "problem children." I took them to lunch acting as normally as possible and decided I'd sit at one of the tables with them instead of walking around, and I'd buy some ice cream for a snack. Perhaps I was just overly hungry. I also decided I'd go and see our school nurse as soon as I had taken the children to their specialist teacher for my planning period.

At the door of the science lab, I blacked out. The science lab teacher caught me before I fell to the floor. The mother who volunteered to help me during lunch guided the children into the lab while the science teacher half carried me to the nurse's office. My pulse and blood pressure were so wild the nurse could not get a reading.

My principal, fearing I might be having a heart attack, called EMS. My school's emergency procedures immediately kicked in. The secretary notified my husband and Rufina from numbers we must all put on a form at the beginning of each school year. (Later, Rufina told me that her boss said her face was white as could be. At first, she could barely speak. As soon as she could find her voice, she called her older sister and then headed for the door.) My co-teacher from the morning and her aid would combine her afternoon class and mine.

I was conscious when they wheeled me out of the building and, with a weak laugh, said to the secretary, "Well, at least I already have a sub for three days." She told me that was the least of her worries.

By the time the ambulance reached the hospital, I was wired up for EKG, had a saline IV in place and was shaking with cold.

The emergency room doctor (after determining from tests that I had **not** had a heart attack or a stroke) decided to keep me in the hospital over-night for observation. My husband arrived as soon as his principal could get his classes covered. My oldest daughter arrived not long after that. Rufina arrived at the hospital first, and after hearing that I was okay, left again to pick up James from daycare. She returned after she had picked James up from daycare and Julio could get to our house to take care of him.

My cell phone had been in my pocket the entire time. Once I was stable, I used it to call my publisher to tell her I was not coming. When I told her where I was, her response was, "Oh, my God! You take good care of yourself."

I had no other problems during the night, so I was allowed to go home the next day at noon and told to see my regular doctor as soon as possible, which I did that same afternoon. My regular doctor sent me right to a cardiologist. Further tests determined that I had had a "stress" or "anxiety" attack, the symptoms of which can seem very much like a heart attack. I needed rest and less stress. Not an easy thing to do under the circumstances.

James still had to sleep at our house, but we had everything covered for his care. One small bit of paranoia remained: what if CPS decided that my hospitalization indicated that my husband and I were unable to care for James? Would they use that to prolong the case again and place him in foster care? Because we feared the answers to those questions, we decided not to inform CPS about my "incident." Rufina picked up James in the mornings and dropped him at daycare on her way to work. I spent three days sitting on the couch, sipping tea and reading a good book. So many friends called to ask how I was, it amazed me.

I also used the time to compose a letter I had considered writing for the previous couple of weeks. It was time for "push" to become "shove" if I wanted to relieve myself of the stress my entire family was under. I mailed it the first time I was able to drive safely again.

(Our address and phone)
April 17, 2008

Marilyn Thomas, CPS Supervisor, Unit E0
Dept. of Mail Code 182-3
3 Northpoint Dr, Suite 101
Houston, TX 77060

RE: Case Number 200703616J

Dear Marilyn Thomas:

There are several points of the case with our grandson James Bonilla I need clarified as soon as possible.

First of all, let me state clearly, since I have the distinct feeling that CPS is scrambling to cover its backside, I have absolutely **no** intention of filing any civil suit for the incredible incompetence CPS has shown in our case. That is my truth, in spite of the many untruths told to us.

It has often seemed to me that CPS is not concerned with the prompt return of James to his parents because he is "with family" so his parents get to see him often enough. However, being with his grandparents rather than his parents is **not** the same for James. He and his parents have had a year of their lives together effectively stolen from them for no really good reason and with a definite lack of evidence of abuse or neglect.

On 25 Feb. 2008, when we sat in the conference room at the court house, I asked if you would approve Rufina Bonilla's transportation of James to and from doctor/dentist appointments unsupervised. (She and Julio already have court-given permission to transport him unsupervised for other purposes.) You stated that you had no problem with that. I asked if we needed some sort of letter or paperwork for Rufina to show medical people and you answered, "No." Later I felt we **should** have something on paper. On 27 Feb, 2008, you called my cell phone in response to my request for this permission on paper. You said you would be out of town for part of that week but would get right on it when you returned. On 7 Mar. 2008, I left a message on your voice mail because sufficient time had passed and I had not received a letter or fax regarding that permission. On 12, Mar. 2008, you finally returned my call and said that you could not write such a letter until after the forensic team had handed down a decision. This is a contradiction of what you stated to me earlier about not needing a letter and then about getting such a letter to me. So, were you lying in the court house conference room? Or were you lying to me on the phone when you said you would write such a letter? Or were you lying to me when you said you could not write the letter? Only one thing can be true, so two of them are not true and therefore are lies. Which two? I believe I have a right to know the truth. On 25 Feb. 2008, you and Dr. Sharp both said you believed Rufina and Julio Bonilla as to the circumstances of James Bonilla's head injuries. You said there would be a quick resolution to this case. On 7 Apr. 2008, during your phone call to me, I asked what you meant by "soon" since six weeks had passed and we had no resolution. You stated that, to you, "soon" meant a couple of weeks. You admitted that the problem was that the previous case worker had said she had all the medical records, but had not actually had them. In telling me that, you admitted that the previous case worker had lied to us (and possibly to the court). You said that we should have a decision "by Wednesday" (April 9). On 10 April, you called me again to ask whether I had ever received the $1000 stipend for the Kinship Program. I responded that I had not. You asked about paperwork for it and I stated that all the studies, paperwork, signed, etc. had been completed in November 2007. You said you would check into it. I asked about the forensic team decision. You said it would be "by today" (April 10). When one considers that we still do not have a decision, neither date was the truth. It has now been a full month since I delivered the CT films to Dr. Sharp. So when will this case be resolved? It is very important that I know the truth because I must make decisions **now** concerning upcoming travel.

Later on 10 April, I received a message from Jetera Schultz regarding the kinship program. I returned her phone call about 3:05 PM as soon as I was off duty from the children in my class. She told me that she had received our home study "today" (10 April) and that it was marked "approved" on 9 Feb. 2008, but that we were not eligible for the $1000 stipend because of our income level and the stipend was only for families "just scrapping by." The only thing we were eligible for was daycare payments. I notified Elizabeth Cantu (case worker at that point) on 9 August 2007, of our daycare arrangements for James because I had to return to my teaching position in Houston ISD (I had taken Emergency Family Medical Leave from 16 April, 2007 to 25 May 2007, the end of that school year.) I was told on 9 Aug. 2007 that we qualified for daycare payments but that it would take "a few weeks" to set it up. Between Aug. and when we finally were approved on 20 Mar, 2008, we paid $3875 to the day care. I've been told there is no "back pay" for this. For research purposes I asked Ms. Schultz what a foster family receives per child per month. She said it varies by agency and by the level of care. I asked for a "ball park average." She said about $400 a month or $20 per day. Let's do a little math here. By taking our grandson into our home in the kinship program, we have **saved** the state somewhere between $4800 and $7200 in the **year** we have had our grandson. We've had **our** gas, utilities, grocery bills, etc. increase. Our employers have lost many, many days of our time on our jobs. (And in my case Houston ISD had to pay for a long-term sub, while continuing to pay my salary since I had an ample supply of accumulated personal leave days I'd spent 22 years earning and used from April to May 2007.) We have had to take money from our savings to cover our increased expenses that would have gone into our retirement accounts. But we are not "scraping by" enough to qualify for a mere $1000 from the state in compensation for all this? Something is very wrong here. Why are we penalized because CPS delayed so long in processing the paperwork for daycare payments? Why do family members in kinship programs not have the same financial help for providing the same services (better services actually because no foster family could cherish and care for our grandson as much as we do) that foster families do?

Rufina and Julio Bonilla have complied with every request made of them by CPS. They were evaluated by the Children's Crisis Care Center (4Cs) followed all that agency's recommendations; took parenting classes; underwent psychological evaluation and counseling. They proved to the psychological evaluator and their counselor that they are perfectly normal, sane people with a complete understanding of James's epilepsy. You inspected their home for safety on 14 Mar. 2008, and "passed" on it. Jonas Hunter, lawyer *ad litem*, Frank Santulli, defense lawyer, and DA Lynn Chamberlin had all agreed prior to the hearing of 25 Feb. 2008, that James should be returned to his parents. You seem to be the only one holding up this process. Why?

Rufina told me that a couple who took parenting classes with them, who had **confessed** to abusing their children got custody of those children back even before they completed the parenting course! But a year after James was taken away from his parents, nine months after Rufina and Julio completed their parenting classes, CPS clings to custody of James. Why? I think we have a right to know what you are doing and why you continue to delay this case. I think it is time CPS either admits to the error of removing James from his parents, or presents real evidence of abuse enough evidence that a DA would recommend taking it to a grand jury (which we know you don't have) so why can't CPS let go of this case?

Concerning up-coming travel:

On 31 Mar. 2008, concerned with care for James when my husband and I will travel to New York for our youngest daughter's college graduation, I gave you the name and address of Carlene and Mike Ruffino. We have known Carlene and Mike since they were in high school with Rufina and Julio. They have children of their own, one close to James in age. Mike is James's Godfather in the Roman Catholic Church. We often visit them in Brenham. You told me by phone that this would not be a problem but that a home study would have to be done to approve them and that could take some time. This trip is now less than three weeks away and you have not even contacted the Ruffinos. I want you to know that these are the arrangements we have made, and even if CPS delays in approving them, James **will be** in their care from 7 May, 2008, to approximately 14 May, 2008 (timing depends on whether our daughter finds employment in New York, or returns to Houston with us—in which case we will be driving back in a rental truck with all of her things). For the record, incase you misplaced this information, here is their address and phone number:
(appropriate information had been inserted.)
If this case is not resolved by 30 May, 2008, we will be leaving on an extensive trip to Michigan where Jasper and I both have family. We had to give up this summer trip last year and do not intend to give it up again. We will take James with us. We will travel to Tennessee, to visit our daughter, her husband and our granddaughter either going or coming, depending on which is more convenient for them. We will be in Michigan all of June

and July, with James if necessary. He traveled with us just fine last summer when we went to Tennessee for a week in July 2007 (with CPS' blessing). Our address in Michigan is: *(information inserted.)* The phone number there (cell phone service in that area tends to be spotty at best) is *(number had been inserted)*. We spend a lot of time out of doors but we have an answering machine. We also check voice mail on our Houston number two or three times a week. Email remains the same. If you wish to do your "monthly" visits, (which are rarely done anyway) you will simply have to travel to see us, or you may call the Houghton County Human Services Department at 906-482-0500, and have them send someone out. They will know how to find our address or will call us for directions.

Besides my teaching career, I am an award-winning children's author. I have several book events tentatively scheduled at the request of various summer library programs and local festivals in Michigan. Last summer I had to cancel similar events at great personal loss. Then it was too late to get anything scheduled in the Houston area. Things of this nature are planned well in advance and I cannot wait around for CPS to act on this case. I am not turning them down this summer. My husband is perfectly capable of caring for James when I am busy as he has for the times I have had to travel on weekends during the past year. My retirement from Houston ISD will be effective in June so that I may pursue my writing career full time. This will be every bit as much a serious full-time job as teaching has been. So if CPS still has not given up on this case by August of 2008, the need for daycare will be just as great as it is now. I must be free to do author visits in schools (which may involve travel) work on new projects, meet deadlines for assigned articles, etc.

I hope this letter helps you fully understand our perspective in these matters and the need for you to be more truthful with us. I thought you were sincere on 25 Feb. but events since then have demonstrated to me that you will drag this nightmare out in the same manner as the ten caseworkers who preceded you. After telling us we could call or email him anytime, Dr. Sharp's email of 10 April, 2008, seemed to us to say, "Don't call us; we'll call you."

Sincerely,
Deborah K. Frontiera

CC: Frank Santulli
Jonas Hunter
Lynn Chamberlin
Dr. Sharp
Office of Consumer Affairs
Judge Glick
Letter file saved digitally and for future use with the media

(Quoted from the letter composed by the author and mailed to those mentioned. Author has possession of the signed post cards indicating proper delivery to the recipients.)

———•◦•———

I sent copies by certified mail to all those on the CC list. I made plans to mail copies to the Office of Consumer Affairs, our state senator and representative, various media outlets and anybody else I thought might listen or be able to help and set aside the appropriate addresses if we did not have some sort of response from our caseworker within two weeks.

On April 23, 2008, I emailed Dr. Sharp to find out the whereabouts of the CT scan films. I was afraid they might be "lost" and we would no longer have our "proof of innocence." His reply stated that the films were safe; the forensic team had finished; he was out of town and would get in touch when he returned. He would not state what the forensic team's decision had been either to us, to our daughter or to her lawyer.

———•◦•———

Caseworker number twelve, Solana Hastings-Brooks, called on April 25, 2008 to introduce herself. (If Derek Thorworth's supervisor, who originally insisted upon removing James over Derek's objections, is counted, Ms. Hastings-Brooks was the thirteenth CPS person involved with our case.) She had been given the case "last Thursday." I asked if she had read my letter, since I had a signed copy of its receipt from the post office. She had not. I wondered who signed for it and where it ended up.

I asked for her email and told her I would send a copy of the letter. I also decided to write out the main points of our conversation, since documentation of everything was becoming more and more important. The text of several emails exchanged between us follow.

"**Sent:** Friday April 25, 2008, 8:31 PM
To: Hastings, Solana
Cc: Rufina Bonilla; Sharp, Tyrone; Santulli, Frank
Subject: Phone call of 25 April

"Dear Solana Hastings-Brooks:
"This is to confirm the information we discussed in our phone call of 25 April 2008, concerning my grandson James Bonilla.

1. You said that it is NOT necessary to do a home study of Carlene and Mike of Brenham, TX, for their care of James Bonilla while my husband and I travel to New York for our youngest daughter's college graduation. You will find their address and phone number within the letter copied into this email that I sent certified mail to Marilyn Thomas, which was received and signed for on 18 April 2008.
2. You said that you are a firm believer in family reunification. Well, the 11 case workers before you said the same thing and James is still not with his parents. If you want me to believe you, don't give me any of the same bologna we received from 11 previous caseworkers. Make it happen! It

seems every time we have been told James will return home, we get passed off to another caseworker who then must have "more time" to study the case. This line no longer works for us.

3. You said you would be setting up a home visit. Be aware that my teaching duties keep me at school until around 4 each day. I can make it to my house by 4:30 PM. You should find our address in your files and also the name, address, etc. of James's daycare center.

4. You said you needed a copy of Rufina and Julio Bonilla's lease. I said there was no lease; they own their home. You said you needed something to verify their address. The previous caseworkers, when they were told that the Bonillas were home owners, said, "Oh, don't worry about it." They will not send you a mortgage statement with financial information on it. They cannot erase it all to fax you. The same goes for utility bills and other things with their address on it. Most have financial information that CPS has no business knowing. There should be ample information in their file with their address on it. Marilyn Thomas's report on their home should be there. Also, you have their Texas Drivers' Licenses on file. Look them up. Or go to the Harris County Assessors' Department and look up the registered owners (for tax purposes) of 15007 Rigdale, Houston, TX 77084, and you will find that Rufina and Julio Bonilla are the owners. If you have problems with this, contact their attorney, Frank Santulli . . .

"Other issues:

"Please read the letter copied below very carefully and note all of the problems we have encountered. Make a special note of the list of people who received copies of the letter (for which I have proof of delivery). Note especially the last line of the list. On Monday, I will be mailing copies of the letter, this email, and other related material to my state senator, my state representative, the Office of Consumer Affairs, the *Houston Chronicle*, and other media connections."

Ms. Hastings-Brooks reply, sent Monday, April 28, 2008, with Cc's to the same recipients (with the addition of Marilyn Thomas read):

"Ms. Frontiera:

"Thank you, but it was not necessary to create an unofficial transcript of the conversation you had with me on Friday, April 25, 2008. I am very aware of what was said.

No, it is not necessary for us to do a home assessment on your friends that will be caring for James while you travel out of town for a weekend, but I also asked that you supply us with the information of all adult members of the household including dates of birth, addresses and phone numbers. We will have to include the information in our database.

"I never said that I was a firm believer in family reunification because every case that comes into CPS is not like or ever close to the case involving James. I said that if the goal is reunification, services were completed and it is found appropriate that the child returns home from all parties than I will gladly make every effort to return the child to his/her parents. You included that everyone was in agreement that James be returned home, so I will definitely find out everyone's position and follow through.

"In your daughter's and son-in-law's plan of service that was submitted to the court, it requested that they show proof of stable housing, regardless if they rent, lease, or own. "Mr./Mrs. Bonilla (are) to provide copies of the lease/rent agreement to the caseworker no later than 15 days of his lease agreement".

"I will be happy to speak to your daughter and/or her attorney to notify them that we do not need financial records or personal information, but we need a statement letter or even the bottom detachable part of her mortgage statement. And I very appropriately explained this to you on Friday that she can provide us with a cut off portion of her mortgage statement that

simply says her name and the address and that would be fine too. I do not need to do anything further. I will be contacting your daughter and son-in-law, because I am sure that they can handle this as they have been doing well with addressing everything else. *(bold hers)*

"I am not like every other caseworker and I am not like Marilyn Thomas. I was under the impression that our phone conversation on Friday was pleasant but apparently you are still very upset about what someone else in this agency has done. I am sorry if you have been dissatisfied with the way this case went, but the ones hurting from this entire thing are James and his parents. Just because you may have had bad experiences with CPS throughout this case does not mean that I am the same individual that you have been dealing with in the past. I do not need a second supervisor in this case, so I ask that you not accuse me of doing the same to you as everyone else has done before me. I am not new to this job or this field.

"One thing that many individuals do not understand is that it is also the courts decision whether children remain in care or are returned home, CPS caseworkers or supervisors are not above the law, CPS is a witness in front of the court just as relatives and parents are.

"I will be visiting James in daycare, so if you could please provide me with the address of his daycare I would appreciate it."

(It is interesting to note that this caseworker deferred to the courts again when Ms. Thomas had stated that she "had the power" to return James to his home.)

———•◦•◦•———

I replied to her email at 8:56 PM on Monday, April 28, 2008:

"Dear Ms. Hastings-Brooks:

"You may not feel it is necessary for me to unofficially document the contents of a phone conversation, but I do. Twenty-three years in Houston ISD have taught me to document everything. I do similar notes every time I talk with a parent of one of my students. It keeps me knowledgeable of what was said because sometimes memory fails. If this offends you, I'm sorry. I have such unofficial documentation of every conversation with every caseworker we have had. That is why my letter to Marilyn Thomas was so accurate as to what occurred between Feb. 25, 2008 and the date of the letter.

"I have given you, or other case workers on several occasions the name and address of James Bonilla's daycare. In case you have lost it, or that paper is missing from our file here it is again at your request: *(information followed)*

"I usually drop him off between 6:35 and 6:45 AM and pick him up between 4 and 5 depending on whether I have after-school meetings, traffic, etc. Rufina picks him up about 5:20 PM on Wednesdays and Fridays (with court permission—this should be in his file, if not, Westwood has copy of the court order giving parents permission to do this.)

"I do not personally know Mike and Carlene Ruffinos' birthdays. Carlene graduated in the same class as my daughter Rufina, class of 1995. She has been married a couple of years longer. There are no another adults living in their home that I am aware of. You may call them at *(phone number inserted)* They will answer any questions you may have for them that they feel are appropriate once you explain to them the need for that particular piece of information.

"If you feel I am judging you based on the work of previous caseworkers, remember that the eleven caseworkers who came before you made numerous errors (missed deadlines, missed court dates, missed meetings, lost case files, constant delays) which have pro-longed this case unnecessarily. This, unfortunately for you, makes it more difficult to change our perception of CPS, or for us to believe that you will accomplish more than you predecessors. Each time we have had a new caseworker or supervisor assigned, that person has had to take more time to become familiar with the case and this has prolonged things even more. In my many years as a teacher I have often had students assigned to my class whose parents have had unfavorable experiences with a previous school or teacher. It was up to me to prove to them that I was different. You are now in a similar position.

I appreciate your taking time to respond to my email and look forward to a new beginning."

(Quoted from printed copies of the author's own emails.)

———•◦•◦•———

Rufina went to the Harris County Appraisal District's web site, looked up her address with its tax information, printed it and faxed it to Ms. Hastings-Brooks to satisfy the requirement of proving their address, (even though that same address showed on their driver's licenses, and the previous caseworker had been to their home).

I received polite replies from the Office of Consumer Affairs, but no action that I was aware of ever took place. I also received polite replies from my state senator and representative. Much later, my state representative asked for more information, but nothing came of it. Rufina and Julio received a polite letter from the Office of Consumer Affairs that Senator Kay Bailey Hutchison's office had forwarded their correspondence to that office. Each letter stated that such matters were in the hands of the courts (which we had already discovered follow CPS's lead in any case). We had seen, and heard, Ms. Thomas state that she had the power to return James to his home. Such "buck-passing" continued to prolong our case.

I sent Dr. Sharp another email on May 1, 2008, once again asking the whereabouts of the CT scans of 20 February 2007. I received a reply that he had returned them to Cypress-Fairbanks Medical Center. I placed a call to that institution to make sure and was pleased to find out that they indeed had the films back in their files. No one from CPS had at that point had the courtesy to tell us what decision that CPS's forensic team had made.

It wasn't until May 6 (one day before we were to leave James with Carlene and Mike) that CPS called Carlene. All CPS wanted was to verify their birthdays.

—•◦•◦•—

CHAPTER NINE

And Just as Suddenly

Our trip to New York was a mixed bag of emotions. Our pride in our youngest daughter floated over an underlying current of stress. We crowded into my sister's tiny apartment grateful to have a free place to stay. Our oldest daughter stayed in Jamie's dorm room since her roommates were not graduating that year and had already left. Graduation day dawned cold and misty. We arrived early in the outdoor area on Pratt's campus which had been set up for the ceremony and found good seats. Before long, the cold mist turned to rain. Jasper found some ponchos for all of us before they sold out, and we huddled under umbrellas. Before long, hundreds of umbrellas popped up, each keeping its holder dry but dripping onto people next to, in front of, or behind. The wind picked up, and it rained harder. As we peeked from beneath a scaly roof of umbrellas, trying to catch a glimpse of our daughter during the processional, my husband commented, "Think on the bright side. James could be here, too." We couldn't help but laugh at the thought of our super-active grandson climbing all over chairs and laps if he had been with us.

We caught sight of Jamie, walking proudly in her cap and gown, rain and all. She didn't put on the plastic poncho issued to her until she had reached her seat.

Unfortunately, the wind increased and the rain came down harder, forcing college officials to abbreviate the ceremony. They conferred degrees *en masse* and dismissed the sopping wet crowd without a recessional. We were far too cold and wet to attend the reception, choosing to go to Jamie's dorm room to take pictures and get dried off before leaving the campus. All of us (my husband and I, our oldest and youngest daughters, my sister and her daughter and grandson) went to a market area along the Brooklyn docks to have lunch. The place had a lovely view of the harbor, but we could barely see the Statue of Liberty through the rain. If spite of that, we were a happy group.

The following morning, with the weather much better, we headed for Battery Park. Jamie had purchased reserved tickets in advance for the ferry to Liberty Island and Ellis Island. It turned into a very special day for all of us. On Sunday, we broke into pairs. My oldest daughter had bought tickets to a show on Broadway, her Mother's Day gift to me. Jamie and Jasper (since he has never been a fan of musicals) went off on their own, taking in the Empire State Building and Ground Zero. He offered to help load up the rental truck which Jamie would be driving back, but she insisted on her independence. She did allow him to highlight the best route in a new highway atlas and promised to call every evening of her long drive home.

Not until our last evening in New York did we allow ourselves to discuss what lay ahead with CPS and James. My sister's advice was to continue to pressure "the powers that be" and take back our lives and, as we had also decided, include James in all our plans as if the situation would be permanent, but do what we wanted to do. We returned to Houston with a true feeling of acceptance of whatever occurred.

Meanwhile in Brenham, Rufina had taken Friday off to help Charlene with her youngest and James because Charlene's oldest was participating in Mayfest that weekend. Rufina felt more relaxed and was glad to talk things out with Charlene, make phone calls to prepare for the retirement party she and her sister were planning to throw for me, and found she could "just be normal" for a weekend. They played inside with the kids on Sunday and went to dinner to celebrate Mother's Day. By then it was getting late and Rufina and Julio knew they had to return to Houston. James was having so much fun with Charlene's children that he was okay with her leaving him. Rufina was not doing well at all. She looked in the rear-view mirror while driving down the street and ended up in tears before she turned onto Highway 290. For a second Mother's Day, she had to drive away from her child through no fault of her own.

Monday, May 12, I sent Ms. Hastings-Brooks another email, outlining our plans for summer travel with James, providing exact dates, addresses and phone numbers. I asked once more to know CPS's intentions concerning the case, reminding her that we had not had the "required" monthly home visit since February, but stating firmly that nothing her agency did would change our travel plans. I did not receive an immediate reply.

Around 4:00 PM on Monday, May 19, 2008, Ms. Hastings-Brooks called my cell phone. "We're letting James go home this week. What day and time would you like?" and then she said, "I'll be calling the mother next."

Just like that!

No explanation. No "We finally believe you, sorry for turning your lives upside down for thirteen months." Certainly no, "Sometimes we actually make mistakes." No mention of having to go to court first. Only the simple announcement that they were now letting James go home.

I was so taken aback I can't recall the first thing I said, but I requested Wednesday after school, so we would have time to gather all James's things. I waited a few minutes before calling Rufina.

"Have you picked up your jaw?" I asked her.

"What?"

"Didn't the caseworker call you?"

"Yes, but I couldn't pick up my cell phone."

"Well, you better call her back. They're sending James home! Wednesday at 4:00 PM!"

"What!"

By thirty minutes later, she had sent out a mass email with the good news.

———◦•‡•◦———

Ms. Hastings-Brooks arrived promptly at 4 PM on Wednesday, May 21, 2008. She wanted to take James in her car, but I informed her that he would never get into a stranger's car without someone he knew and we had already loaded most of his things into my vehicle. I suggested she follow me since she did not know where Rufina and Julio lived (because she had never visited their home) and traffic could be heavy.

Only after James was hugging his mommy and daddy did I gather enough courage to ask what had finally tipped things in our favor.

"Well," Ms. Hastings-Brooks said, "I read the file and could see there was nothing there. So we had a staffing and I asked why we were still keeping this child."

I managed to keep my mouth from dropping open and thanked her.

Read the file.

What a concept!

———◦•‡•◦———

CHAPTER TEN

Afterward

The following Saturday at James's third birthday party, he hugged me at first, then backed away and clung to his daddy's leg. Sunday at church he cried when I tried to hug him, fearful I suppose, that I would not let him go home with his parents. I understood his feelings of distrust and backed away. I went out to their house a few days later to drop off a few toys we'd found behind the couch. James was fine with me being at **his** house. When I said good-bye, he took my hand, walked me out the door to my car, practically pushed me in, and then waved as he watched me back out.

Two days after that, as soon as I had finished the last of my paper work at school and had been honored for retiring at a luncheon my school's PTO puts on each year for teachers on our final work day, my husband and I left on our summer trip—by ourselves. It felt like a second honeymoon.

June 16, 2008, Rufina called to say it was "officially" over. She expressed her sentiments clearly in a follow-up email to friends and family:

> "Well, we went to court today, and the case is officially over. CPS non-suited out of it (meaning in the eyes of the court this case NEVER happened). All we got from the judge was a congratulations . . . It took all of 2 seconds to end 13 months of HELL.

Deborah K. Frontiera

"James is adjusting although we are still going through the separation anxiety stage again. When we are at home he does not want to let us out of his sight, and when we are going somewhere he fears that we are taking him back to Grandma and Grandpa's house. We started potty training because he was showing signs of being ready, but we had to give up for a while because he did not want to cooperate. We think maybe in his own way he is trying to get back that year and just wants to be our baby which is fine. We know eventually he will adjust and feel safe again."

July 29, 2008, she wrote:

"James still won't be a big boy and use the potty. We can now be in a different room than he is, but he makes sure we are still there every once in a while. He still needs an item of security when he is dropped off at daycare; however, if he brings five trucks from home, we can leave all but one in the truck. There are still times, though, when he will have a temper tantrum because he can't bring any more than that inside, and then he clings to me when I leave. He is talking more and more. Two weeks ago I was lifting him out of the tub and said, 'Oooh, what a big boy.' He replied, 'I baby.' I told him, 'No, you are a big boy,' and he again replied, 'I baby.' . . . Also around that time he started wanting his door left open when we put him to bed, and then a few nights ago he would not stay in bed unless we lay down next to him until he fell asleep. It's like in some cases he is getting better, but in others he is regressing. We'll see what happens when Mom and Dad return from Michigan next week—whether he'll want to run and hug them or shy away because he'll be afraid they'll take him from us. We took him to see Aunt Jamie, who is staying at their house, a few weeks ago, and he did not want to let us out of his sight. Maybe that is what started this whole thing at night."

(Above two letters quoted from Rufina Bonilla's emails and used with her permission.)

James was shy with us when we first returned to Houston. We let him have his space. It was October of 2008 before he really wanted to come into our house. But in November he hopped gladly into our car when we strapped in his booster seat for a trip to McDonald's after church. But it wasn't until March of 2009 when we were able to take him for a day trip without his parents to Moody Gardens at Galveston during spring break. We had a wonderful time with him and only the Rain Forest Pyramid was still closed due to damage from Hurricane Ike the previous September.

A year later, we were still receiving the monthly letters for eligibility for Medicaid, in spite of the fact that we had written and called several times to inform that office that James was back with his parents and on their private insurance so there was no more need for continued Medicaid eligibility letters. The state "First Steps" office, which makes sure children in CPS custody have regular medical check-ups, continued to send us letters asking why he had not been taken to their approved doctors, even though I had called more than once to say James was no longer in CPS custody, was on private insurance, and his pediatrician and neurologist (whom he had been to see) were not on their "approved" lists. Apparently, they had still not read the file or paid attention to my previous calls and letters. Rufina related that the daycare continued to be paid throughout the summer of 2008, right up until James began the PPCD program in Cypress-Fairbanks ISD. (She regarded it as a small pay-back for all the months they were supposed to pay and hadn't.)

The same day that the judge formally returned James to his parents (June 16, 2008), Frank Santulli, our lawyer, filled out the paperwork requesting a complete copy of all the court's records. Months went by without the court informing him that the records were ready. In December of 2008, he put more pressure on them to get the copies of the records ready for him to pick up. It wasn't until April 22, 2009 (ten months later and two years after the start of our nightmare) that he was able to pick up the records: over 200 pages, for which the court charged over one dollar a page to copy.

I read through them page by page comparing them to the records we had been given along the way. Rather than quote the documents in their entirety, I am listing only the differences between the official Court Records and the documents and medical records we had. I will leave it up to readers to form their own conclusions about what these differences imply.

A court employee, Belinda J. Chagnard, had issued a subpoena to Dr. Michelle Lyn (the Texas Children's Hospital doctor who signed the papers originally accusing Rufina and Julio of child abuse) to appear in court on April 25, 2007 (the date of the Show Cause hearing). It was not delivered. The subpoena had "unable to serve" written on it. There was no follow up paperwork. Dr. Lyn never appeared in court. On the copy of her original statement to the court, her signature and printed name were clearly readable. On the copy given to us, neither her signature nor her name could be read easily.

Rufina also had told me earlier that spring that they had seen someone named Dr. Lyn on a Houston TV news broadcast saying that head injuries were the leading cause of death in children. A child had pulled the cord of a TV set, which then fell from the top of a dresser onto his head. The child died. (Obviously a tragic accident and not abuse.) Dr. Lyn didn't state on TV her opinion as to whether that was a case of abuse/neglect or not. Many children have accidents that result in head injuries that are not due to abuse or neglect, but she certainly had judged our grandson's case hastily and in error.

A subpoena for James's medical records from Texas Children's Hospital was delivered and the records were accepted at the Court House by Judith Gibson. Neither we nor our lawyer ever saw or spoke with her.

On February 25, 2008, CPS filed a report with the court concerning the Permanency Plan and the progress Julio and Rufina had made on their Family Plan. The date of an earlier report (October 29, 2007) was crossed out and the date February 25, 2008, was hand written over it. It was identical to the report CPS filed with the Court on October 29, 2007, and did not mention that Rufina and Julio had completed all requirements stated in their Family Plan, including going to individual counseling, by the February date. There was a hand written note about changes in James's medication with a new date written over the older one and a note about initiating steps for the PPCD program. There were no initials or signature as to who made these hand written changes.

There were several bills to The Court for the services of Jonas Hunter, James's attorney ad litem:

$150 for appearing in court on April 16, 2007; $250 for court appearance on April 25, 2007; $150 for court appearance on October 29, 2007; $150 for court appearance on June 8, 2007; $150 for court appearance on June 20, 2007; $150 for appearing in court on February 25, 2008; and $150 for appearing in court on June 16, 2008.

(Quoted from copies of original court documents obtained by the Bonilla's lawyer and now in the possession of the author. Used with Rufina Bonilla's permission.)

Mr. Hunter spent less than ten minutes at our home on one day near the beginning of our ordeal. None of our court appearances took longer than twenty minutes and some hearings took even less time. The "trial" on June 16, 2008 had lasted less than two minutes. There were no bills from Mr. Hunter for any work on James's case outside of the courtroom and no indication, from our perspective, that he did any other work on James's behalf. We observed that he appeared at court in multiple cases for other children on the same days that we were there—presumably with similar fees billed.

The court order of February 15, 2008 granting an extension to CPS in our case extended it until October 17, 2008. (CPS could have dragged our case on until that date.)

Court papers on June 8, 2007, finally replaced Derek Thorworth's name (the first case worker involved) with Katieka Bonner's name (the fifth case worker assigned to us). There were notations made about changes in status with "the parents" and several "has not" sections had been crossed out.

Papers filed by Mona Ellis, custodian of records for the Children's Crisis Care Center, in a deposition filed on July 18, 2007, stated: "Family might benefit from review by Interdisciplinary Team to have an objective opinion regarding the nature of James's injuries so that they can fully accept that James was mistreated and in need of protection." No where does it state whether "they" refers to CPS or to Rufina and Julio. As stated earlier, this review by an Interdisciplinary Team (which was supposed to be made up of doctors not connected with any of the parties involved CPS, Texas Children's Hospital or James's regular pediatrician) never did take place. CPS only reviewed their own files with their own medical review, the one for which they never provided us a copy or news about the report.

Among papers on February 25, 2008, some stated that James was in a "medical facility" and other stated that he was "placed with the maternal grandparents."

There were several differences between the medical records Texas Children's Hospital gave The Court and those they gave to me (even though I had requested "all" records and had been told that was what I had received). There was a physical abuse check list with a diagram of the body of a child, front and back, for a doctor to indicate where there were injuries, bruises, etc. Nothing on the list was checked off and there were no indications on the body diagram of any bruises, and plenty of references to how "normal" James's development seemed to be. One note recorded Rufina and Julio's 6:15 PM arrival on April 13, 2007, with the indicator "suspected NAT" (non-accidental trauma). They had not even been interviewed at that time about any explanation of his injuries. There were hand-written comments by someone on April 13, 2007 on Rufina and Julio's behavior during interviews at the hospital. These notes mentioned that Julio became "diaphoretic" (which means he broke out in a sweat), but no one asked him about this. (Julio sweats constantly and wears shorts and T-shirts outdoors even on Houston's winter days when temperatures are in the 40s) and that "the parents seemed agitated" while later additions stated they were "calm and cooperative."

(Selected paraphrased quotes in the paragraphs above are from the court documents obtained by the Bonilla's lawyer and later given to the author. They are used with the Bonilla's permission.)

I had to wonder about the statement "the parents seemed agitated." Wouldn't any parent, called and told to go immediately to the emergency room because something had shown up on an MRI, be "agitated?" Rufina and Julio were agitated that day because they feared that what showed up on the MRI might be cancer or something worse they couldn't even imagine. (An MRI shows much more of the brain and its blood vessels, etc. than the simpler CT scan, which is an elaborate x-ray.) They were also agitated because they had fought their way through rush hour traffic only to sit and wait for two hours and discover that no one would explain anything to them. Whoever made this notation certainly wasn't taking any of their feelings into consideration hardly good "bedside manner" for hospital officials. Had what showed up on the MRI been a cancer, I would bet hospital officials would have acted much differently, or at least I hope they would have.

A 10:16 PM note told of a "red mark" from James's fall in the waiting room. Pages and pages of hand written notes stated in timed intervals whether James was sleeping, awake, active, blood pressure, temperature, etc. during his hospital stay.

A note on April 4, 2007 by a Dr. Robert Zeller stated that Rufina had called after the EEG earlier in April to ask that James be put on anti-seizure medication immediately. (She had called, but only to find out the results of the EEG.) At one point, CPS had brought up the idea that Rufina might have Munchausen Syndrome by Proxy where a mother keeps saying a child is ill, or making the child ill, to get attention for herself. (Perhaps Dr. Zeller's, and other similar notes, in the Texas Children's Hospital records given to The Court, and we assume to CPS but not to us, were the reason for that ridiculous suggestion.)

The hospital records given to The Court (but not to me or to James's parents) contained references to the referral to CPS with orders not to discharge James to his parents at times before anyone had notified Rufina or Julio that they were "suspected" child abusers. A social worker's report we had never seen was also included. Also noted was the negative CT scan from February showing no injuries at that time (which Dr. Megahed had told me, after the date The Court had received these records, he did not have access to). All of these differences were hand written and not included in the neatly typed versions given to me.

Court records show that these medical records were signed and witnessed by a Notary Public on May 9, 2007. They were entered in Court Records as "Exhibit A." (Months later, CPS was still claiming they did not have James's medical records.)

The formal document from the June 16, 2008 hearing filed by CPS to The Court stated only the obvious: CPS's original reason for removing James from his home; the fact that Rufina and Julio had done everything CPS had asked; that Rufina and Julio now seemed to understand James's special needs and were now capable of caring for him properly; that James had been returned to his home.

Nothing was entered in the official record concerning the Interdisciplinary Committee (which never took place even though The Court had ordered it). The final document also mentioned nothing about CPS's own medical team which had supposedly met and decided based on James's medical records, whether or not there had been abuse/neglect. No report from that forensic team was included, even though Marilyn Thomas and Dr. Sharp had made such a point to state to us that such a review had taken place, and we must wait for the results.

(All short quotes and paraphrased descriptions are from the documents obtained by the Bonilla's lawyer. The documents are now in the possession of the author and are used with Rufina Bonilla's permission.)

The discrepancies in the official Court Records made us wonder what other errors might exist in CPS's case file on James. Rufina made an official request for a copy of their entire case file on April 27, 2009, along with a statement that she would pay whatever copying charges there were. She received twenty-seven pages of records in June of 2009, but only with her name on them. She had to make a second, separate, request for their file on Julio.

CPS's case file on Rufina was more significant for what it did not contain than for what was there. We had expected to see copies of transcripts from the Permanency Planning Team meetings, copies of reports that should have been filed concerning the few home visits caseworkers did make to our home, a copy of the home study done on Rufina and Julio's home, progress reports the agency had to file with The Court, the reports from Walker Counseling concerning the psychological evaluations, and other such documents Rufina and Julio should have had a right to see. None of those were in the twenty-seven pages given to us. There also was no report from CPS's own forensic team. Either Rufina was not given the entire file she requested, or those reports never existed, or perhaps CPS "accidentally lost" large portions of the file because those documents might have made the agency look bad.

———◆◆◆◆◆———

PART II

Was Our Case Atypical?

In our case, no police were involved. No real investigation ever took place. No caseworker ever visited or called James's baby sitter. Dr. Lyn, who signed the affidavit, never questioned Rufina or Julio beyond the questions regarding auto accident and fall from a great height. No doctor (that we were aware of at that time) at Texas Children's ever used a computer mouse to check the results of the EEG available within Texas Children's Hospital's own records. No one from CPS or Texas Children's Hospital ever questioned James's regular pediatrician as to whether he had ever seen any signs of abuse (which he would have been obligated to report if he had seen such things, and hadn't reported because there was no such evidence). No one from CPS or Texas Children's Hospital (that we were aware of at that time) requested records from Cypress Fairbanks Medical Center **before** removing James from his home even though his parents signed several releases at various points while James was still in the hospital. Neither the doctor, nor any representative of the hospital, ever came to Court. The supervisor who overruled Derek Thorworth in his belief that this was not a case of child abuse or neglect never answered our messages and never came to Court. Rufina and Julio Bonilla were never given the opportunity to confront their accusers.

No legal rights were read to or presented to the Bonillas at the time CPS took their child from them, or at any other time. Indeed, neither they, nor any parent, have any legal rights under the "Family Code" of law in Texas because these proceedings are done in Civil rather than Criminal Court. An accused murderer has more legal rights than a person accused of abuse/neglect of a child. The State of Texas only moves a CPS case to Criminal Court when they have actual evidence that will stand up to a criminal prosecutor's scrutiny. Even later, the Bonilla's lawyer was not given the opportunity to question any of the people responsible for removing James from the custody of his parents since those parties never appeared in court.

We were told this is because it is all about the safety of the child. Rufina and Julio were kept "in the dark" in the hospital emergency room because many abusers take their child and run (or do not seek medical attention at all until it is too late for the child) because they fear "the system." As one example of this, the *Houston Chronicle*, in an article "Another Child, Another Missed Chance?" stated:

> "Amber's parents—Hobert Maccurdy and Melissa Menkes—along with maternal grandmother Linda Menkes, have been charged, accused of failing to seek medical attention leading to Amber's death. They didn't seek medical care, her mother told authorities, because she was afraid Texas Child Protective Services would take Amber and her two brothers away from them."

(Houston Chronicle, *Sep. 9, 2009, Pg. A-1. The author subscribes to the newspaper and retained the clipping from her copy. This short quote falls under "Fair Use" laws.)

CPS and hospitals resort to the kinds of tactics used on us to trick parents into staying. Because of other high-profile child abuse cases not long before ours in which children had died of abuse, CPS had taken the stance of assuming the parent or caretaker was guilty of abuse and removing the child using an "immediate danger" clause in the law which allows CPS to act in this manner. The system then demands that parents prove their innocence beyond any possible doubt. CPS assumes guilt and doesn't investigate the possibility of innocence. Only later, if CPS decides to involve the police and moves the case to criminal court, do a person's legal rights and the "presumption of innocence" apply. Sadly, in the case quoted above, (*Chronicle*, Sep. 9) CPS had had previous chances to remove the child from the home and had not.

Anytime a child dies as a result of abuse, it becomes headline news. Three such cases happened shortly before and after our case began. One child had been placed in a microwave oven and "cooked." One mother had cut off her child's genitals and blamed it on the family dog. Other cases continued to make the news in the months immediately following. In one instance on May 29, 2007, Fox TV News reported that a child died of burns after being immersed in scalding water. The mother took the child out of the scalding water in the bath tub only when her skin began to fall off. The report stated that in such hot water the child had to be screaming in pain. The mother was reported to be "afraid" to take the child to a doctor because CPS had taken her children away before. She waited a few days before seeking medical treatment. The child died as a result of the burns. Cases such as these, and the resulting criticism of CPS in Harris County, probably contributed to CPS insisting that our grandson be removed from his parents.

(The author subscribes to the newspaper and retained the clipping from her copy. This information above falls under "Fair Use" laws. Articles have been paraphrased by the author.)

I don't fault CPS in their efforts to protect children. I do understand that they had reason to investigate our situation. I know that when Rufina and Julio told doctors, "He falls down a lot," it probably sounded suspicious. *He/she falls down a lot* is probably the number one excuse of parents who really do abuse their children. In the same way, teachers hear *the dog ate my homework* and think,

"Yeah, and I have some ocean front property in Arizona for sale." But, in truth, some children really do fall down a lot, and some dogs do eat homework.

What was wrong, very wrong, was CPS's total lack of real investigation; their incompetence along the way; their dragging out the case for over a year (perhaps in some desperate move to "save face" for their many errors) and their inability to say, "We're sorry. We now see that this was a medical problem and realize you were doing your job as parents, but we have to do our job, too." We could all have accepted that.

Children's Protective Services does, indeed, have a difficult job to do.

They just do it very badly.

I collected clippings of news articles in the *Houston Chronicle* during the entire time our case was in progress. The file grew to one inch in thickness. The worst cases always seemed to involve children whose parents, step parents, and guardians were involved with drugs or alcohol.

While everyone, including me, agrees that children must be protected from abuse when it is really happening, it should not be the "right" of agencies to overstep their power by taking children from families with no proper police investigation or supporting evidence. Children and their extended families, like ours, become additional victims, all in the name of protection.

Another part of CPS's difficult job is that no one can know ahead of time if or when a person will crack beneath the strain of parenthood, job loss, or poverty and act out by hurting or killing a child. Many families exist "beneath the radar," in that they continually move from one neighborhood to another, change schools, or move from one state to another whenever someone begins to suspect they may be abusing their children. No one has a crystal ball to predict the future. CPS caseworkers have been criticized in some cases for failing to remove children from abusive adults and in other cases for failing to return children who are not in danger of abuse or neglect.

Anonymous calls to child-abuse hot lines are important to have, but they can be misused by angry ex-spouses or ex-lovers, disgruntled employees, autocratic bosses, overly nosy neighbors, or anyone to "get back at" someone by calling in an accusation of abuse. In the same way, real abuse cases can sometimes be ignored because of frequent false reports.

I believe that only a tiny portion of "false" abuse allegations ever come into the public's knowledge.

No names or locations are revealed in the cases discussed in this section unless the people involved gave their permission, or unless they are quoted from public sources. This is to preserve the privacy of those involved so they need not fear any possible repercussions as a result of speaking to me. Where there are obviously fake names, the information presented cannot be independently verified because I will not provide the names of those involved. Dates of newspaper articles (similar to the one already quoted) or books follow accounts from those sources. Web information is included where appropriate.

<hr>

Case I

I n a case in Florida, Children's Services had taken a child away from a Cuban-born father declaring him an "unfit" parent and placed the child in foster care.

The case became bogged down "in a legal maze of what makes a father a fit parent and in lawyerly definitions of abandonment and neglect." When a judge finally ruled in favor of the father, another legal battle began. The child had been with foster parents for so long that the then-five-year-old girl had formed a strong emotional bond with the foster parents. They claimed it would be detrimental to the child to be taken away from them and returned to the father because of this bond. The judge in the case had a new problem to solve that brought up a constitutional conflict in the State of Florida: "Does his right as a fit and loving father to raise his daughter trump her right not to be torn from a family she has come to love?"

This is also a clash of cherished American principles: "the constitutional right of a fit parent to raise his child free of government interference vs. the government's right to protect a small child from potential emotional harm."

Bernard Perlmutter, who heads the University of Miami Law School's Children & Youth Law Clinic stated, "We are treading on very dangerous borders of the law. We have to be very careful."

"The Florida Department of Children & Families, together with the girl's court-appointed-guradian-ad-litem, are asking

Miami-Dade Circuit Judge Jeri Cohen to forever strip
Izquierdo of custody over his daughter by granting her foster
parents permanent guardianship. They say the girl has so
completely bonded with her half-brother and foster parents
that separating from them now would endanger her
emotionally."

It would appear that one state agency is trying to create new
jurisprudence focusing on potential harm to a child. Florida law
at the time offered little guidance or precedent for the case.

"Bruce A. Boyer, a law professor who leads Loyola University's
law clinic in Chicago, called 'really, really scary' the notion that
a fit parent can be deprived of his child. 'Before a state can
interfere with the relationship between a parent and child, it has
to first establish that something has gone wrong.'"

(Houston Chronicle, Sep. 29, 2007, pg. A 12. The author subscribes to the
   newspaper and retained the clipping from her copy. This short quote falls
   under "Fair Use" laws and has been paraphrased by the author.)

I have to wonder in this case why the child was removed
from the home in the first place, why the case took so long to resolve,
and why the father was unable, or not allowed, to have regular
supervised visits with his daughter in order to maintain his bond
with her. The report I read did not provide any of these important
details. Possibly, the reporter on the story wasn't allowed access to
both sides of the story. I also wonder if some of the delays in the
case resulted from caseworker incompetence, constant change of
caseworkers or other problems similar to those we encountered. It
is one thing for parents who divorce to argue in court over custody
issues, but quite another for a state to take a child away from a parent
who was declared "fit" by courts in that same state.

———•◦•———

Case II

In another case reported in October of 2007, an Asian family accused CPS in Houston of not understanding their culture. Martha Wong, a former state representative from Houston who had become involved with the case had stated, "Asian families take care of Asian families; it's in the culture."

The case involved a child whose mother had schizophrenia and occasional angry outbursts. The child was being cared for by his grandmother and an aunt when his mother was hospitalized or off her medication. CPS became involved in 2005 when it was reported that the child was not being adequately cared for. The grandmother, who was in Houston, and the aunt, who was in Arizona at the time, often ferried the child back and forth between them. They stated that translators from CPS misunderstood them, and that they always kept the boy safe. Kim Szeto, with Asian American Family Services, and others believe CPS is not sensitive to the insular nature of Asian families and that Asian families, in turn, are not always savvy in the way they deal with the agency.

CPS stated that the agency does provide adequate translators, has Chinese and Vietnamese caseworkers, and cases of abuse/neglect cross all cultural boundaries. They also stated that they do try to keep children with family when possible, but that they didn't feel that the grandmother and aunt were doing an adequate job of protecting the child. Estella Olguin, spokesperson for CPS, was quoted in the *Houston Chronicle* as stating: "(Mental illness) is not just a stigma with the Asian community. But the fact that they would place their grandchild or their nephew in danger because of their denial of it or because it is a stigma, that is what is concerning and made us worry that they would not protect Raymond in the future." CPS prevailed in court convincing a jury that the child belonged with Anglo foster parents, not with his mother's family.

> The battle in court lasted three weeks and polarized the Asian community in Houston. Asian American Family Services formed a fund called "keep the family together" to help provide lawyers for the boy's family and others fighting battles with CPS.

(Houston Chronicle, Sat., Oct. 6, 2007, City/State section. The author subscribes to the newspaper and retained the clipping from her copy. The report has been paraphrased by the author. This short quote falls under "Fair Use" laws.)

In September of 2010, I followed up on this case with a phone call to Kim Szeto at the Asian American Family Services, asking her if the appeal had succeeded. Ms. Szeto graciously gave me a good bit of her time on the phone. She said that the case still saddened her. The appeal had gone no where and the child was lost to his mother and her family forever.

Because of the publicity the case received, there were several blogs about it all over the world. The *Houston Press* and other media did extensive stories. Both young lawyers and experienced, well known attorney Gary Pollen became involved with the case. Ms. Szeto was present at the trial and could tell that the court-appointed interpreter was not doing an adequate job. Members of the child's family spoke a different dialect than the interpreter. There were many times that words were misinterpreted. Ms. Szeto felt that had made a great difference in the case, resulting in the family losing this child. She also felt that CPS had not done a proper job of investigating the case from the beginning. The Asian American Family Services organization hired a special interpreter to listen to and read the trial transcript. That specialist came to the same conclusion: misinterpreted words had lost the case for the family. But even that didn't help on appeal. The child has been lost permanently to his family.

Ms. Szeto told me that when the child's mother stays on her medication, she understands that she no longer has custody of her baby, but sometimes when she doesn't take her medication, she becomes confused, calls a taxi to drive her around from one place to another saying she is searching for her baby.

Ironically, after all the publicity, Ms. Szeto was appointed to the CPS board in Houston and participated in training sessions for caseworkers to help them become more sensitive to Asian culture. Since that time, the Asian American Family Services has received many more referrals from CPS.

———•·•·•———

Case III

I became personally involved in another case in Houston shortly after I retired from teaching in Houston ISD in June of 2008. At first, the mother involved wanted me to use their names so that someday her children would understand the circumstances and why their mother ultimately had to relinquish her parental rights voluntarily in order to get her children out of the foster care system and back with family members. Later, she thought it best to remain anonymous.

During that last chaotic year of teaching, I had a little girl in my class, T1. Bright-eyed and always with a smile, she was an absolute delight to have as a student. Even at age four, she could print her entire first and last names with ease. T's mother, E1, was a single parent and working full time, so I did not see her often at school, but spoke with her frequently on the phone in the evening. Sometimes I called E1 to report good progress. Other times, she called me (during my entire career, all parents had my home phone number and were encouraged to call me) asking advice about good daycare centers or how to support T1's education at home. I would always hear T1's happy voice in the background during these phone calls and usually ended up talking to her, too. It was easy to hear her smile and sense her enthusiasm for life. Whenever her mother was able to come to school for special programs such as parents' night, open house, etc., T1 was with her always smiling. T1 was open, friendly, helpful with other children, and very talkative. She was often the one who got out paper or crayons for everyone while I dealt with another child's temper tantrum.

E1 had immigrated to the United States from Kenya and had left family behind there. T1 had been born in the United States, but an older brother, T2, was still in Kenya living with E1's sister and her husband until E1 could make arrangements for him to immigrate legally and rejoin his mother. T1's father remained "unknown" because her mother had chosen to give birth and keep and love her child even though she was the result of a brief affair and the father was long gone, not even knowing about T1.

Children with family problems often have difficulty in school with behavior or academic growth. They become quiet and withdrawn or overly aggressive. Any change in behavior patterns signals me that I need to talk with the parent about changes or problems in a child's life. Divorce, a new baby brother or sister, and other such things show up in a young child's behavior. Children who are neglected often come to school in less than clean clothes, devour their free breakfast and lunch, are often picked up by older siblings, have poor attendance or are "sick" a lot. Such children usually have poor academic growth and poor social skills. Young children's art work often reflects their problems constant use of dark colors like purple and black and scribbling on top of an otherwise good picture.

I can't begin to count the number of parents I have referred to various social agencies for counseling, finding new housing, reporting domestic abuse, etc. Some problems were solved easily with me telling the parent where to find whatever kind of help they needed. Other times, I involved my principal in finding the right course of action, and, yes, there were times my principal and I called CPS.

Not even once during the school year did I see any "red flags" of family problems, let alone child abuse, in T1.

Close to the end of the school year, E1 called me. She had finally completed arrangements for T2, nine years old at that point, to come to Houston. She wanted to know if she should enroll him in school so close to the end of the year, or wait until the start of the new school year. I told her she should enroll him, even though only about six weeks remained. I said that would give teachers the opportunity to assess his needs to see if he was academically behind due to differences in schools and cultures, or needed to be in an "English as Second Language" class (he spoke Swahili and English). If he needed any of these services, he would begin those programs promptly at the start of the new school year. E1 followed that advice and contacted the school where T2 would go. Brother and sister would not be in the same school because the school where I taught served children only in pre-k through second grade.

E1 told me that T1 would be absent the day they went to pick up T2 at Houston Intercontinental Airport. I kept my eyes open those last few weeks of the school year anticipating adjustment problems between a pre-school girl and an older brother living together for the first time. The fact that T2 would have a huge adjustment getting to know his mother after six years of separation (there had been many phone calls, letters, and photographs but they had not seen each other) plus being in a totally different culture, was not far from my mind. I did not see any significant change in T1's behavior. She remained cheerful, talkative, and said it was okay having a big brother.

School ended and my husband and I left for our cottage in Michigan and a much needed rest. I put the school year's photos in my keepsake drawer and moved on with my life.

In October 2008, I picked up the phone and heard E1's lilting accent. "Mrs. Frontiera, this is E1. Do you remember me?"

"Of course! How is T1 doing in kindergarten? Did she get into the gifted and talented program?"

"I don't know. I need your help. I have no one here except the pastor at my church. CPS took the children away from me."

"What!"

Deborah K. Frontiera

After school was out, T2 had problems adjusting. He had hit T1 a few times. Once he had sprayed her toothbrush with hairspray. E1's pastor had advised her to keep an eye on T2. She had tried. But in late June, she had taken T1 to the doctor for a fall which resulted in a bruise on her forehead. Before she knew what was happening, CPS had arrived at the doctor's office and removed both children. E1 didn't know where they were. CPS wouldn't tell her and wouldn't allow even supervised visits. E1 was told that the children didn't want to see her.

"Have you got a good lawyer?"

"Yes, and he's trying to help, but CPS won't even return my calls."

"You need to document the date and time of every call."

"I have been. It doesn't help. I don't know what to do."

I tried to reassure her, got the date of her next hearing and promised to be there. Later she sent me a copy of her attempts to contact her caseworker. Her formal record keeping had begun on August 11, 2009. She listed calls and messages on August 12, 13, 20, 22, September 4, 5, 8, 12, 15, 23, 24, 25, 26, 29, October 6, 8, 17, 21, 22, 23, 24, 30, 31, November 5, 6, and 10 on the pages she gave me. CPS would not tell her where the children were, who the foster parents were, and continued to state that the children did not want to see her. Of course, the policy of not telling parents where foster parents live protects foster families from possible confrontations with parents who might indeed be violent. CPS would not even allow her to talk to her children on the phone. Knowing T1 as well as I did, I could not believe that she did not want to see her mother. E1 worried that her children thought she no longer loved them. She missed them terribly and had trouble sleeping at night. Fortunately, her employer was understanding and supportive. She continued to work; indeed, she had to with the mounting legal bills.

We had a good chance to talk before her hearing in Court on December 10, 2008. I met her pastor, Stella Alhassan, and the pastor's assistant, Frieda Perkins. Both firmly believed E1 had never hurt her children. They felt that T2 probably had hurt his sister and now was afraid to say so. Stella and Frieda felt that perhaps CPS had filled T2 with fear that he might have to go to Juvenile Court or to jail. He was still in culture shock and may have believed terrible things might happen to him. It was probably easier to say his mother had hit T1. Fear and being in a different country can do strange things to a child's mind. E1 believed T2 would say whatever he thought CPS or the counselor assigned to the children wanted to hear. It had been nearly six months since E1 had seen or talked to her children.

E1 had gone through the assessment at 4 Cs (as we had) completed parenting classes and done everything CPS asked of her. Yet the "primary goal" CPS had listed in her case was "non-relative adoption." I didn't want to worry her at the time, but I considered that a very bad sign. In my eyes, CPS had decided from the beginning to sever her parental rights.

I asked if CPS had ever come to her home. They had not. During that hearing in December of 2008, E1's lawyer managed to ask me some basic questions about my relationship with T1, and I was able to put in a few positive statements before the judge cut off the questions stating that this was only a status hearing, not a "trial." The judge didn't permit the other people there supporting E1 to be questioned either. CPS caseworkers continued to state the goal of non-relative adoption and insist that the counselor working with the children stated that the children didn't want to see their mother and that supervised visits were not in the children's best interests. The counselor was not in attendance at the hearing for E1's lawyer to question her about this subject. The judge accepted CPS's version of the situation. E1 would not be given permission to have supervised visits.

By March of 2009, at another hearing, I learned that the lawyer *ad litem* for the children had not even met with them. How can someone know the best interest of the children if he has not even met with them? Yet this lawyer hired by the court to advocate for the children went along with CPS's and the counselor's continued insistence (again, the counselor was **not** in the court room) that the children did not want to see their mother. The volunteer from Child Advocates, who at least had seen the children, also insisted that the children didn't want to see their mother. CPS still had **not** visited E1's home. Again, the judge denied supervised visits over E1's lawyer's objections. The case was continued until June of 2009.

After court that day in March, I managed to talk to the Child Advocate volunteer, the CPS caseworker and one of CPS's lawyers. The lawyer said he was surprised by my testimony that T1 was bright, bubbly, a happy child who had done well in school. He asked if I would be surprised to know that she was 180 degrees different now, that she kicked and screamed not to go home. I said that would indeed surprise me. I asked if I might be allowed to visit her or talk to her on the phone. They said, quite firmly, that no such visit would be allowed. I gave them all my phone number and said I would be very willing to talk more with them. I was never contacted.

Since I would not be in Houston for the June court date, E1's lawyer had me come to his office on May 6, 2009, to give a sworn deposition. CPS's lawyers, the Child Advocates volunteer and others involved in the case were invited to this deposition so they could question me as well, but only a Child Advocate volunteer (a different person from the one I had met at court in March) came. She asked me no questions. In the deposition, I went into great detail on many things I remembered from the school year with T1, my years of experience, my knowledge of how to know when a child might be having problems, and previous experiences with children who had problems, all to establish that I knew what I was talking about. I stated that I had never seen any signs or signals of abuse, that I had frequent phone conversations with T1's mother, and had often been asked for and given advice.

I gave E1's lawyer a phone number where I could be reached in June and promised to remain near the phone that morning in case someone should want to ask me anything during the court hearing. No one called.

In July, E1 called me. The June hearing had gone like the others. My deposition had gone nowhere. CPS had even referred the case to criminal court. E1 had been arrested for "injury to a child," arraigned and released on bond. The lawyer to whom I had given the deposition was no longer on the case. She had new lawyers, two for the CPS case and another for the criminal case. E1 still felt T2 was scared to admit he might have injured his sister and said, "I have faith in God who knows my hands are clean."

E1's mother, EM, her sisters ES1 and ES2, and brother EB, arrived in December 2009, from Canada, and Kenya to help and support E1 and to try to convince the powers that be to allow the children to live with them. CPS allowed these relatives a supervised visit at CPS offices. It was a good reunion for children and relatives. ES1 told me later that T1 had asked them where her mother was and why she was not allowed to see her mother. This aunt stated to me that T1 had cried at one point because she thought she would be allowed to see her mother. Both children said they loved their mother, but at one point T2 told his Aunt (with whom he had lived for six years in Kenya) "You know, I'm not allowed to say that [Mommy I love you] again." So it slipped out that someone had told the children repeatedly what to say or not say.

EM, T1's grandmother, liked to think of the words, **woman** and **parent**, as acronyms with the following characteristics: **W**onderful worker, **O**ffers herself, **M**aker of her home, **A**ctivator, **N**ever gives up; and **P**rovide, **A**dvise, **R**ebuke, **E**ncourage, **N**urture/ Love, **T**rain. She knew her daughter had done all these things for

T2 during the three years before she had to leave him behind to immigrate to the United States, and for T1.

We met at Court once again on December 14, 2009. T2 had been taken to the hearing on that day by his foster mother. He saw his mother, aunts and grandmother in the hallway and immediately approached with hugs and smiles. E1 saw her son briefly for the first time in eighteen months. Her eyes were filled with tears. He was smiling. To me, this did not look like a child who had insisted he didn't want to see his mother. CPS and T2's foster mother whisked him into a conference room away from his family. T1 was not in court. I approached the three volunteers from Child Advocates and asked about her. They acknowledged my concern and thanked me but were tight-lipped except to say she was doing well in school.

In the hall outside the court room that day, E1's lawyers and CPS worked out a "deal." If E1 voluntarily relinquished her parental rights, CPS would allow her sisters to adopt her children. T1 would live with her Aunt ES2 in Canada and T2 would go back to Kenya with Aunt ES1, who had cared for him previously. This, of course, was subject to the governments of Canada and Kenya doing their version of "home studies" to be sure that these women would be proper parents. Until those studies took place, the children would remain in foster care.

The county attorney, arranging all this for CPS, answered her cell phone in the middle of the discussion of this "deal" as we stood in the hallway outside the courtroom. She put her phone to her ear and said, "I can't talk right now. I'm in the middle of a trial."

E1 saw T2 out in the hall again and got in another hug. He was confused and upset that he would not be going home with his aunt that same day.

E1's lawyers persisted in their requests for assurances that CPS would follow up and be sure the children did indeed go to these family members. While CPS stated this would be the goal, they also stated that there were no "guarantees." I watched as E1 stood before the judge declaring that this was her signature on the forms; that she understood what was happening; that she was indeed doing this voluntarily. I felt everyone present knew, as I did, that E1 had no choice. If she wanted to get her children out of the foster care system, if she wanted to be able to talk to them, write to them and visit them in the future, she had to give them up. How ironic that a mother must "give up" her children in order to be able to see them.

EM, E1's mother, commented later that it was so unfortunate that things had not gone well when T2 joined his mother and sister after so many years apart. She was dismayed that "the law of the land" would force a separation between parents and children before offering real help and support. She knew that E1 felt there was no alternative to giving up her children and that she did it out of love for them so they could be with family instead of staying in the foster care system or being adopted by strangers. She was grateful to God that she had been able to travel from Africa to be with her daughter at such a trying time. "It was painful to watch my daughter being prosecuted as a murderer or a dangerous criminal, but we understand it is the Rule and the Law of this land America. God searches the heart and knows the truth, and we pray that one day the truth shall come out to the open and my daughter E1 shall be set free by her maker who is the almighty God," she told me later.

Inside the courtroom, E1's lawyers pounded on the counselor, who was actually present this time, making strong arguments for E1 to be able to have supervised visits with the children based on what had occurred that day in the hall. The counselor conceded that things may have changed since the family visit the pervious week, but she and the volunteer from Child Advocates still seemed to want to control the situation. It was apparent they had some mutual understanding or agreement with each other in spite of what all of us had seen that day between T2 and his mother. The judge stated that both children should be brought to court so that he could talk with them privately one at a time.

E1's mother gave me another statement later about what her daughter had been, in effect, forced to do: "She did it for the law and rule of the land. She did not sign out that they [T2 and T1] did not belong to her own womb; that she didn't carry them for nine months in her womb; that she did not go through labor pains as any woman does; that they were not born to her; that they did not suck her own breasts; that she did not give them life. I thank God she gave them life. I pity E1 for what she has gone through and is still going through. I love her so much and I know she is a God-fearing woman, who loves her children very much and prays for them day and night. I know for a fact that God will reward her and the truth shall be known someday. I know there are rights that nobody can remove through life or death. May God bless America and all the innocent people who are suffering for crimes that they did not commit."

E1 called me after Christmas. Her sisters and mother had had another good visit with the children, but she had still not been allowed to see them. The children never did go to talk to the judge. Family members felt they would be afraid and would only say what the foster parents, the therapist, and the Child Advocates volunteer told them to say, which would not be the truth. E1 also told me that my name had been mentioned to T1. She remembered me with love.

On August 17, 2010, nearly nine months after that court date, I was privileged to accompany ES1 to one of the CPS offices in Houston. I was able to visit with both T1 and T2. T1 was the same bubbly girl I remembered not a 180 degree different child described by the lawyer. I was able to hear from T1 directly that there had been a time when she felt "afraid" to see her mother, but she now longer knew why. Perhaps she had heard too many things from her foster mother, well-intentioned but untrue things, about what her mother might do. Perhaps she was simply afraid of the whole situation and what might happen next. Perhaps, because she had never been allowed supervised visits, phone calls, or letters from her mother, she was afraid her mother no longer loved her. Whatever the reason, she wanted to see her mother that day.

T1 did get to see her mother that day, and it was a very joyful reunion. It was the first time they had been able to see each other in over two years! It was very evident that there was a lot of love there.

ES1 was given full custody of T2 that day—no more CPS involvement. Period.

ES1 hoped that, since things were still bogged down with Canadian authorities completing the work for T1's Aunt ES2, CPS might give her custody of T1 as well. But T1 was not sure how she felt about that. To go with her Aunt ES1 would mean leaving **everything** behind that she knew home, friends, school, even her country a very scary thought for such a young child. During a trip to MacDonald's to get some lunch (in my car) ES1 told her to tell the casework supervisor, the judge, her therapist, and everyone what she truly wanted from her own heart not to listen to what others told her to say. "You should be with your family," she said. "I love you; we all love you. I want to be your 'Mama ES1', but even I shouldn't try to tell you what you should do. Talk to God. Listen to your own heart."

When we left the CPS office at the end of the visit, the casework supervisor promised to "work on it" for T1 to be able to see her mother again. E1 expressed the hope that, since T2 was now "free," she would be able to free T1 from foster care as well. A month later, after ES1 and T2 had left for Kenya, E1 was still not allowed to have supervised visits with T1. The next hearing date was scheduled for January of 2011.

———✦———

Case IV

In the late 1990s, Mr. Z's step-daughter married a man whom Mr. Z described as not a good husband or father. The child's babysitter suspected there might be sexual abuse of the child and reported it to the child's mother, who took action. She filed for divorce and tried to get full custody. A criminal investigation took place, and there was enough evidence to take the case to a Grand Jury. But because many women claim abuse by a former spouse falsely, the Grand Jury "no billed" the case. Mr. Z's daughter continued to try to work through CPS to get full custody and restrict access to the child by the father.

Mr. Z was an "outside observer" in the case, always there to support his step-daughter emotionally but not directly involved. He noted that the child's father had unlimited funds for a "better" lawyer, while his step-daughter, with less money available to her, had less effective representation. Mr. Z noted the conduct of all the lawyers during Family Court proceedings. They seemed "too cozy" with each other in his opinion, bantering around before court started, as if they were best buddies, had already reached an agreement outside of court and were only waiting for the judge's "stamp of approval." The lawyer for his step-daughter's ex-husband constantly disparaged his step-daughter, accusing her of being the one at fault, and making the child's father the "victim." This lawyer also used "not ready" tactics to delay and delay the case so that it took over a year to settle.

Mr. Z felt that the bantering and joking about by the lawyers was unprofessional behavior and questioned how invested they were in the case. After all, once settled, they would have no more income from those particular clients, so what was their incentive to conclude the case quickly? Mr. Z felt that the CPS caseworkers involved seemed sensitive to the child involved and to his step-daughter. He also noted that they were very young, inexperienced, and ineffective when cross-examined.

Ultimately, Mr. Z's step-daughter prevailed and won full custody with the child's father ordered to have no further contact with the child or the mother. In return, no charges were filed against the father. Whether the records were sealed or purged, Mr. Z did not know. He and I were acquainted through a professional organization. I noticed the same coziness and banter among lawyers every time I sat in a Family Court Room.

———◆·❉·◆———

Case V

ACPS caseworker visited an elementary school to check out an anonymous tip about Child A, enrolled there in pre-school. School administrators were stunned. While they had, over the years, called CPS because they suspected some children were abused or neglected, an accusation concerning Child A surprised them. The child was not absent more than "normal," didn't arrive tardy very often, was clean and well-dressed upon arrival, and they had not seen any bruises. Administrators sent the caseworker to talk to the child's teacher.

Child A's teacher was also surprised by the accusation. The teacher was, however, aware that Child A had some special needs. She had been working closely with the child's mother concerning Child A's wild mood swings, tantrums, and other social adjustment problems. Child A's mother had taken her to various doctors and the tentative diagnosis was that Child A had Attention Deficit Disorder and was suffering from bi-polar disorder. They were having difficulty finding the right medication to help the child. Child A's teacher told the caseworker that she had seen no signs of child abuse and accepted the caseworker's card.

Later, Child A's teacher realized what an outsider, unfamiliar with the child's medical problems, might think if they heard one of the child's tantrums through the thin walls of apartment buildings. She wrote these thoughts in a letter to the caseworker to follow up on the case. Later, she heard from Child

A's mother that CPS officials did visit her apartment, found it to be safe, relatively clean, and found no signs of abuse. Two months later, CPS was still "keeping tabs" on the family, but made no attempt to remove Child A or her siblings from their home. Child A's mother thought that the apartment supervisor may have been the one who reported her. She had filed complaints against the apartment management company because they failed to properly clean mold from apartment air ducts.

This is one case of which I am aware where the system worked the way it should. It is also a case where CPS actually investigated a situation before removing children from a home. Whether the anonymous tip came from apartment management or from a neighbor with valid but misinformed intentions is not known. Knowledge of the case came to me through a trusted teaching colleague.

❖•❖•❖

Case VI

Ex-Mrs. Q and New-Mrs. Q became better acquainted when New-Mrs. Q began telling Ex-Mrs. Q certain incidents concerning daughters, C and D, born to Ex-Mrs. Q and Mr. Q during their marriage. C and D were ages eight and four at that time and the divorced parents shared custody. New-Mrs. Q's first call was to tell Ex-Mrs. Q that the children had witnessed some very harsh fighting between her and the father, and she was concerned about how the girls would understand it. Ex-Mrs. Q felt her daughters' stepmother genuinely cared for the children; and she was somewhat glad of the many conversations that followed because she now knew for certain that she had not been "crazy" in her reasons for her own divorce. She told me, "Someone else was now living my marriage." But the conversations were disturbing, too. Arguments, blow-ups and make-ups continued for several months between the girls' father and stepmother.

Summer vacation arrived. Ex-Mrs. Q and her new husband took the girls for a two-week camping vacation and then delivered them to Mr. Q and his wife for two weeks, during which Mr. Q and his wife took the children on a large cruise ship. When the children came home to their mother, they behaved terribly. C went through her box of "dress-up" clothes and danced provocatively. D sat in her mother's lap and then bit her nipple, through her clothes, as they read a story at bed time. Both girls acted "snotty" toward their mother and stepfather.

Ex-Mrs. Q met for coffee with New-Mrs. Q the following morning. New-Mrs. Q was concerned again because the girls had witnessed her fighting with the father during the cruise and had explanations for their behavior. C and D's father had taken the girls to the "shows" on the cruise (something both mother and stepmother had asked him not to do) and encouraged them to act like the dancers. Mr. Q had also begun a "game" with the girls and had told them to bite his nipple and said it tickled. He had also insisted that the girls sleep with him. He did not sleep with his wife but was "intertwined" with the girls. This type of behavior had been the start of many fights between Mr. Q and New-Mrs. Q.

Ex-Mrs. Q, encouraged by another friend, reported the information to CPS in the state and county where they lived. CPS initially took the case seriously and came out for a home visit. However, it took a **month** of excuses before the caseworker returned to interview C and D. When the caseworker did talk to the girls in September (spending over half an hour with each girl) it was as if a great weight had been lifted, but another one put in its place. The caseworker was adamant that Mr. Q was grooming C, that the girls knew their roles, and that there should be no more unsupervised visits until counseling had taken place for all three of them. The girls revealed to the caseworker that C, the older of the two girls, had taken showers with her father. The caseworker stated to the girls' mother that he thought their father was really sick and needed counseling, and that the mother and step-father should be their only supervisors. He also stated that if Ex-Mrs. Q had not reported the incident, CPS would have been investigating her for not protecting the girls. Ex-Mrs. Q took notes about the conversation (and all subsequent conversations) immediately afterward. Ex-Mrs. Q took the CPS caseworker's advice, got a new lawyer who dealt with such cases, went to court and managed to get a temporary restraining order.

During this time, New-Mrs. Q had assured the girls' mother that she would support her in going to court over Mr. Q sleeping with the girls. But when it came time to actually go to court, the girls' stepmother back-pedaled and said it really wasn't all that big a deal; she supported her husband, Mr. Q, not the girls.

Mr. Q scheduled supervised visits with D but not with C, the older of the sisters. Instead, he broke the restraining order and went to the children's school to have lunch with C, claiming that teachers were around he didn't need a supervisor. Ex-Mrs. Q called the sheriff. Shortly after, Mr. Q's lawyer asked the girls' mother to "back off" so he could get the case dropped. She declined.

In October during court, Mr. Q blamed all of it on his ex-wife. He stated in a letter that the girls needed all the love and physical affection they could possibly get from him. He wrote that they were starving for affection because their mother and step-father ignored them and that D spent all day in a daycare where she got no attention at all. He seemed to believe what he wrote.

The CPS caseworker, who had interviewed the girls and been so insistent that they were being groomed for future sexual abuse, now believed their father's statements, not the girls he had so carefully interviewed. In spite of all his previous statements, the caseworker gave Ex-Mrs. Q nothing: not a letter for the court, not a word that confirmed what the caseworker had said again and again—that the children's mother and stepfather were doing the right thing, that they **had** to report it, and that if the girls' mother had **not** reported the incidents to CPS, she could have been charged with not protecting the girls.

In Court, Mr. Q's response to the "nipple sucking" (which D had cheerfully described to the caseworker) was that the girls were into nipple sucking because their mother played that game with them at home. He constantly pointed fingers in other directions.

The judge stated that without some statement or document from CPS, he could not change the shared custody arrangement or their parenting plan. The hearing became a case of "he said/she said." However, the judge spoke almost entirely to Mr. Q. in his admonitions and restrictions. Mr. Q was not to shower with the girls, sleep with them or engage in any "nipple games."

CPS closed the case. The caseworker and his supervisor refused to meet with Ex-Mrs. Q so she could ask him how he had come to the conclusion that CPS should not remain involved after his statements upon interviewing the girls.

The girls' mother wrote letters to supervisors on the next level up. Neither the caseworker nor his supervisor would meet with Ex-Mrs. Q. She felt they had back-peddled and betrayed her and the girls. Her letters to the supervisor were not acknowledged. Her calls were not returned. She wrote to the governor of her state, who replied that she should write to the CPS Area Administrator. She did so and requested a copy of the files. She was told it could take "up to thirty days" to get copies of the file. The following February, she still had received no reply to any of her letters or calls. Ex-Mrs. Q wondered how a caseworker could "decline" to meet with a reasonable, questioning client. The area administrator responded to her letters, but still they did nothing. No meeting between the girls' mother and the caseworker ever took place. No copies of the file were ever sent.

Knowledge of this case came to me through the friend of a friend in the state other than Texas.

—•◦•◦•—

Case VII

On July 17, 2002, the U.S. 5th Circuit Court of Appeals outlined the constitutional relationship between social workers and families. The report of the case, Roe v. Texas Dept. of Protective and Regulatory Services, appeared in the *Handbook for Home Texas Schoolers.*

"The landmark case . . . centered on the unconstitutional strip and body cavity search of one Jackie Row, a six-year-old girl, by Barbara Strickland, a CPS caseworker. The basis for Strickland's search was information received from an anonymous hotline call, which led CPS to believe that the child might be suffering from sexual abuse. Ms. Strickland then made contact with Jackie's mother and scheduled a meeting at the Roe household. Strickland did not, however, inform Mrs. Roe of the purpose of the visit. . . .

"Mrs. Roe, though uncomfortable with the demands of Ms. Strickland, reacted passively, so Strickland proceeded. After taking the photographs [of the child's private parts] Strickland interviewed Jackie and then left. The investigation was then dismissed, and no allegations of abuse were lodged by CPS.

"The U.S. 5th Circuit Court of Appeals held that Agent Strickland's actions were inexcusable. Nevertheless, the court granted Strickland qualified immunity because it was not clearly established at the time of the strip search (and this Strickland could not have known) that the 'special needs' doctrine did not allow social workers to conduct warrant-less strip searches of children. . . .

"The 'special needs' doctrine states that 'Public officials can justify warrant-less searches with reference to a 'special need' 'divorced from the State's general interest in law enforcement.' Examples of this doctrine include a principal's search of a student's desk for drugs in school, a public employer's search of an employee's desk, and drug testing of U.S. Customs Service employees applying for positions involving drug interdiction. It was Strickland's position that her warrant-less search could be justified under this special needs test. . . . The Court ruled that the 'special needs' doctrine did not allow social workers to conduct warrant-less strip searches of children. . . .

"A social worker must demonstrate probable cause and obtain a court order, obtain parental consent, or act under exigent [urgent or critical] circumstances to justify the visual body cavity search of a juvenile."

(Handbook for Texas Home Schoolers, *2008-2009, Texas Home School Coalition Association, PO Box 6747, Lubbock, TX, 79493, www. THSC.org, 2008, pages 2-14 and 2-15. Quoted with permission.)*

———•◦•———

Case VIII

Mr. YZ was married for several years and divorced. This marriage had produced a daughter, D-1. He became involved with Ms. M and quickly realized this was not a woman he wanted to spend his life with and prepared to move on. Ms. M wanted him to marry her, so she allowed herself to become pregnant. (Many months after, another family member would find a notebook in which Ms. M had written, "He's such a good father, but he won't marry me, so I'll get pregnant.") Mr. YZ still broke off his relationship with her, but intended from the start to be financially responsible for another child. When the baby, another girl, D-2, was born, he went to the hospital to see his child and immediately gave Ms. M legal paperwork and began to send child support checks. He also wanted some kind of a relationship with this new daughter, so he filed papers with the court for regular visitation.

A few months later, Mr. YZ began dating a woman that he knew he did want to marry. This woman became close to D-2 during Mr. YZ's regular weekends with D-2. Around the time they became engaged, Ms. M realized that she had truly lost Mr. YZ. She apparently felt that since she couldn't have him, she would set about to make his life miserable by filing a report with CPS claiming that he was sexually abusing D-2. It was quite a shock the first time a CPS case worker showed up at Mr. YZ's home to investigate this accusation.

Mr. YZ and his fiancé hired a lawyer and proceeded to prove their innocence. An independent physician quickly determined through a complete physical exam that no sexual abuse had ever taken place. CPS dropped the case against Mr. YZ two months after it was filed which had been in August of 2006.

Ms. M moved to an adjacent county and in December of 2006, filed another complaint with CPS in that county. Mr. and Mrs. YZ again found themselves accused of child sexual abuse, and statements that their home was not safe for the child. This time they had to appear in court in a different county. They tried to file a counter suit charging Ms. M with filing a false report and quickly learned that they could not file a suit against Ms. M while there was a CPS case pending against them! They obtained a subpoena for all of D-2's medical records to discover that on every Monday following a weekend the child spent with Mr. and Mrs. YZ, Ms. M took the child to her doctor, complaining that she was sick, had a rash, or some other medical problem, always saying that the child had picked up whatever complaint it was while with her father. D-2 did have some breathing problems, so there was some concern about her health.

On one visitation weekend, D-2 arrived at Mr. and Mrs. YZ's already ill. D-2's father and stepmother were diligent about her care and reported to Ms. M when they brought D-2 back to her mother the symptoms they had seen and what they had done. This illness was also blamed on Mr. YZ when Ms. M took the child to the doctor that Monday.

During the second court case, Mr. YZ had a subpoena sent to this doctor. Under questioning, the doctor stated that he had never said to Ms. M that he thought the child had been sexually abused and that none of the "Monday complaints" had amounted to anything serious. More money and lawyers later, this second case was also closed by CPS workers in the county where Ms. M then lived.

By this time, D-2 was three years old. When Mr. and Mrs. YZ would arrive to pick up D-2 on their weekends, she would seem happy at first to see them. Then she would look at her mother and begin crying and carrying on. On one particular trip when D-2 was finally out of sight of her mother's house, she said, "Can I be happy now? Mommy can't see me."

Mr. and Mrs. YZ felt they were constantly "watched" and that even the smallest questionable action on their part would result in another complaint to CPS by Ms. M. She would make them wait outside if they arrived to pick up D-2 at 5:50 PM instead of the arranged 6 PM, and would criticize them if they were even five minutes late due to traffic returning D-2 home at the end of the weekend.

Mrs. YZ began to study the issue of "Father's Rights" and found a web site with lists of what some women do to get back at former husbands or boyfriends. Ms. M had done several of the things listed. They wondered if Ms. M had found this site as well and used it as a set of directions. During the months that they were under investigation by CPS, their lawyer had advised them not to pick up D-2 for regular visits. The constant stress of paying lawyers fees, going to court, not seeing the child, etc. caused a huge strain on Mr. and Mrs. YZ's marriage, but they were determined to rise above the situation and not give up their right to be involved in D-2's life.

They even complied with CPS's request to take parenting classes when there was an issue of being too harsh with "time outs" at times when Mr. YZ had visits with D-1. They found that with each CPS complaint, new caseworkers were assigned to them. Caseworkers were also changed during the course of a case, even the ones that lasted only two months. They would have to answer the same basic questions over and over with each new person involved. Most caseworkers seemed very young, inexperienced and not well educated. Some seemed intimidated by Mr. and Mrs. YZ's education and knowledge of their own rights. Mr. and Mrs. YZ often heard caseworkers speaking with poor grammar and found spelling mistakes in agency forms and documents, actions they felt were highly unprofessional. They noted that caseworkers often dragged things out, missed deadlines, and made serious errors in legal documents.

They also found that CPS caseworkers often arrived at court unprepared. Judges did not seem to mind this. But Mr. YZ had to be sure he was more than prepared because judges seemed to expect more of those "accused." Mrs. YZ wrote constant letters to state offices who were responsible for watching over CPS, trying to get the agency to look at the whole picture and the pattern of false accusations in two different counties.

They tried every available legal way to stop the false charges from occurring. Police, district attorneys, their own lawyers—all said that there was no action that could be taken in their state against Ms. M's constant barrage of false charges. While filing a false police report can result in criminal charges, a false report to CPS carries no penalty at all in most states. It was apparent that Ms. M could do whatever she wanted. Mr. and Mrs. YZ had no recourse. One person advised that the only thing they could do was turn around and file a CPS claim against Ms. M!

"I wouldn't do that to my worst enemy," Mrs. YZ said. Indeed, why would they want to heap more emotional pain and confusion on D-2? Somehow, they had to continue on the high road.

At one point, they discovered that Ms. M had inserted a recording device in D-2's teddy bear. A problem with their telephone uncovered a tap on their phone, which they felt sure Ms. M had somehow arranged although they had no proof. The mental strain grew worse and worse.

An even darker time came in February of 2007. Ms. M accused Mr. YZ's teen-aged nephew of molesting D-2. CPS and police arrived at the teen's school and actually arrested him! They also put Mr. YZ's other daughter through questioning about what her weekends with Dad were like, what they did, where they went, etc. Fortunately, D-1 was old enough to speak for herself and let those questioning her know that she had never been molested or abused while with her father.

This nephew had never been at Mr. and Mrs. YZ's home when D-2 was there. In all, three children would undergo emotional stress and trauma due to Ms. M's false accusations. The nephew underwent the humiliation of being arrested on false charges in front of his friends and teachers. D-1's friends would often ask her in embarrassing ways who the lady was who always came to talk to her. D-2 never knew what to say or how to act with anyone, what would make her a "good" girl, and what wouldn't. She was confused by the months that sometimes went by without seeing her father and did not understand what was going on.

At one point, Mrs. YZ met with Ms. M's father and convinced him of the truth of the situation. But he still stood by his daughter in court against the nephew. When the truth concerning the nephew came out in court, Ms. M's father did not deny that he had talked with Mrs. YZ. Ms. M admitted that she had "heard" that Mr. YZ's niece had visited them one weekend when D-2 was with them. She had made the assumption that the nephew must have visited as well. Mr. YZ's lawyer requested that D-2 be questioned while not in her mother's presence. Ms. M began yelling that she would not allow that. Fortunately, the judge allowed the questioning to proceed. When away from her mother, D-2 freely admitted that, "Mommy told me I would be a good girl if I told people Daddy and (name-intentionally-left-out) touched me on my potty."

Ms. M also admitted, while under pressure under oath, that she had had a personal friendship with a counselor to whom she had been taking D-2, and this counselor had also coached the child on what to say and told her she would be a good girl if she told people that the teen and Mr. YZ had touched her in a sexual way.

The case against the nephew was dismissed. However, that young man will have an arrest record and the shadow of being accused of a sexual crime against a child that will follow him all of his life. Because many people have preconceived notions about those accused of sexual crimes, he may find there is discrimination against him when it comes to applying for a job, living where he wants to and almost every aspect of life.

The nephew's parents decided they would file a civil suit against Ms. M for defamation of character, false accusations, slander, no factual evidence, and mental anguish to their accused son. After they had paid to file the suit and paid a lawyer quite a sum to represent them (who had checked to make sure that particular court had jurisdiction in the case) the judge threw the case out saying the case should have been filed in the county where Ms. M lived, not in his court and his county should not have jurisdiction in the case. The teen's parents decided it was not worth the time and money involved to re-file the case. Once again, there were no consequences for Ms. M.

By this point, proving their innocence time after time had cost Mr. and Mrs. YZ over $25,000 in legal fees, not to mention the stress and mental anguish. Ms. M always seemed to find a lawyer who would represent her for free.

Mr. and Mrs. YZ began to realize they had only two options: try to get full custody of D-2 or walk away from her completely. They had a consultation with yet another new lawyer, one who was very successful at winning custody battles. His retainer alone was $10,000. He told them he could win full custody for them, but in all honesty, Ms. M would be granted visitation rights. They would still be faced with the same ongoing issues and probably more complaints to CPS by Ms. M against them. They decided not to hire him and represented themselves against Ms. M in yet another case.

In the final court battle, Ms. M and CPS wanted to deny all visitation rights for Mr. and Mrs. YZ. Mrs. YZ kept writing notes to her husband to object, or not, and on what grounds. She did such a good job that at one point the judge told Mr. YZ that his "lawyer" was sitting right next to him. CPS tried to say that there was still a case pending against them with the nephew. When Mr. YZ handed the judge the letter stating that the case had been dismissed (something CPS should have known, but hadn't read the notice) Ms. M's facial expression showed such intense anger and shock that she slammed her hand on the table. That made some of the months of agony Mr. and Mrs. YZ had been through seem a tiny bit worth it. They won against Ms. M's attorney and CPS claims. The judge granted them continued visitation rights.

While they still have the right to visit D-2, they have voluntarily chosen not to exercise these rights because they have come to realize that Ms. M will not stop filing false accusations and there is nothing they can do about it. They have chosen not to put D-2 through any further emotional trauma and walked away with their dignity, innocence proven. As of September 2009, they had not seen D-2 for two and a half years. She was by then six years old. They send gifts and cards for her birthday and Christmas, but do not think the gifts are given to D-2. Mrs. YZ began a journal that she writes in frequently "talking" to D-2 about how special she is to them and how much they care about her and what they would have liked to do if they could be together. They know that when D-2 reaches her eighteenth birthday, it will be her choice to visit them and Ms. M will have no say in the matter at all. They have copies of every court document, their letters, and the journal to show D-2 as an adult the truth about how much they cared.

Mr. and Mrs. YZ also have faith that D-2 will one day seek them out. Why? Because Mrs. YZ also sought out her father at age eighteen. They are still involved in D-1's life and both mothers regularly receive child support payments.

---

*Due to the malicious nature of the mother complaining in this case, I will not even reveal the state where this case took place, nor how I came to know about it. I can think of no better case than this to show the need for criminal penalties for **knowingly** filing a false report, or multiple reports with no clear basis, with CPS. Caseworkers should also be more alert to patterns of false reports against certain individuals.*

Case IX

M r. and Mrs. AB had several daughters. One of them, perhaps because of "birth order" had issues as a "middle child," seemed more challenging than the others. During her middle school years, Middle Child and another girl were involved in an egg throwing incident in the neighborhood. Mr. AB, who would not tolerate such behavior, made Middle Child go with him to the house she had egged, apologize to the home owner and clean up the mess she had made. As middle-school-aged children often will, Middle Child "mouthed off" to her father. He reacted with a firm, but not abusive, slap to her face, saying, "Shut up. I'm talking here."

Middle Child apologized to the home owner and cleaned up the mess made by the egg she had admitted throwing. Mr. AB marched her home. It happened that the home owner involved in this was the mother of the other girl involved. She did nothing to discipline her own daughter, entered her house after Mr. AB and his daughter left, and called police to report an incident of child abuse. Within a half hour of her call, a police officer knocked on Mr. AB's door wanting to talk to Middle Child about the alleged child abuse. Within fifteen minutes of talking to Middle Child in his patrol car, the police officer determined that this was not child abuse and returned Middle Child to her home. He told Mr. AB that he could see clearly that this was not abuse, but he was obligated to report the incident to CPS, so they should be expecting a caseworker to call.

A caseworker did come to Mr. and Mrs. AB's home within a few days, found nothing amiss, but suggested some family counseling. Mr. and Mrs. AB agreed since handling teens and preteens could often be challenging, some counseling couldn't hurt and might help. A counselor from a local non-profit agency contacted the family and conducted counseling sessions in their home for several months. The counselor would conduct discussions with the whole family and then speak to the girls without their parents present. She also quickly determined that no abuse was taking place. At one point she told Mr. and Mrs. AB, "I can easily tell that your girls are not abused. They are too quick to tattle on each other and easily share whatever is happening with you. Abused children are usually withdrawn and will not tell what their parents are doing. I really enjoy coming to your home. You people are so **normal**."

Fortunately, the girls were never removed from this home and CPS closed the case. However, cases like this remain in CPS files labeled "unfounded." This can often come back to haunt families years later because "unfounded" usually means that while Children's Protective Services could not substantiate any abuse, they also do not state that the family is "off the hook," and continue to keep the file in their records. They can come back at any time there is the least hint of a problem with that family. The accusation is never cleared from the records.

In this case, the initial investigation was done by a **police officer**, who knew the difference between discipline and abuse. It points to the possible advantage of having law enforcement, not CPS, conducting an investigation. This was a Texas case.

Case X

Perhaps no CPS case was more controversial (in addition to being reported all across the country) than when Texas CPS workers, accompanied by police and several busses, entered (several newspaper reports used the word "raid") and removed approximately 416 children from Yearning for Zion Ranch not far from San Angelo, Texas on April 3, 2008. The ranch was owned and run by a break-away Mormon sect: The Fundamentalist Church of Jesus Christ of Latter Day Saints. The raid was prompted by an anonymous phone call in March from a sixteen-year-old girl who claimed to be living at the ranch, "married" to a fifty-year-old man she claimed beat and raped her. This began a huge and complex court battle.

> "Beginning April 3, dozens of officers searched the compound for six days, seizing cell phones and computers, and eventually forcing their way into the massive alabaster temple while sect members prayed inside. . . In court filings, CPS officials described 'a wide-spread pattern and practice . . . in which young, minor female residents are conditioned to expect and accept sexual activity with adult men at the ranch upon being spiritually married to them.' . . . Laws about polygamy and underage sex apply to everyone with no exception for a religious group. One lawyer described the raid as "stretching probable cause to the limits."

(Houston Chronicle, *April 13, 2008, A-8 and paraphrased by the author. The author subscribes to the newspaper and retained the clipping from her copy. This short quote falls under "Fair Use" laws.)*

"Child welfare officials are ripping open a Pandora's Box of legal, and logistical issues. First looms the inevitable collision between a state's duty to protect Texas children from abuse and the constitutional rights religious liberty and freedom from unreasonable search and seizure. . . On a more mundane level, will be enormous court room management problems."

(Houston Chronicle, *April 13, A-1, paraphrased by the author. The author subscribes to the newspaper and retained the clipping from her copy. This short quote falls under "Fair Use" laws.)*

"There is plenty of authority in the family code to kick in the door if you have a credible report of abuse," said Jack Sampson, a family law expert at the University of Texas School of Law in Austin. But terminating parental rights requires a far greater burden of proof than needed to raid the compound and temporarily remove children . . . and each child will need at least one lawyer. . . you'll need dozens of judges if the state is going to try these cases."

(Houston Chronicle, *April 13, 2008, A-8, paraphrased by the author. The author subscribes to the newspaper and retained the clipping from her copy. This short quote falls under "Fair Use" laws.)*

Dick DeGuerin, who represented the Branch Dividians in 1993 stated:

"It's a classic case of arrest first and investigate later. They took 500 people (some mothers accompanied their children) away from their homes to a make-shift prison without any evidence they've done anything wrong. Child abuse is a bad thing. We need to police it and punish it, when there is evidence it happened. But you can't just say, 'These are Fundamentalist Mormons, they believe in polygamy, and therefore we'll arrest them all and find out if they've been doing it."

(Houston Chronicle, April 13, 2009, A-8, paraphrased by the author. The author subscribes to the newspaper and retained the clipping from her copy. This short quote falls under "Fair Use" laws.)

Things got worse for the women and children removed. On April 15, 2008, they were moved without public notice from Fort Concho National Historical Landmark to the San Angelo Coliseum. There, 392 children and eighty-two mothers of children ranging from newborn to four years of age, were crowded into small areas, cribs and beds placed side by side. Twenty-four teen-aged boys were taken to an undisclosed residential facility. Some women returned to the ranch, leaving their children behind. State District Judge Barbara Walther had to get together with several lawyers to begin to work out several legal issues before they could even have a hearing.

Several mothers wrote a letter signed by three who claimed to represent the rest, asking Governor Rick Perry for help.

"We were contacted and told our homes had been raided, our children taken away with no explanation, and because of law enforcement blockade prevent [ed] entering or leaving the ranch, we were unable to get to our homes and had no-where to go. As of Wednesday, April 9, 2008, we have been permitted to return to our empty, ransacked homes, heartsick and lonely. . . Many of our children have become sick as a result of the conditions they have been placed in. Some have even had to be taken to the hospital. Our innocent children are continually being questioned on things they know nothing about. The physical examinations were horrifying to the children. The exposure to these conditions is traumatizing them."

(Houston Chronicle, April 14, 2008, A-4. The author subscribes to the newspaper and retained the clipping from her copy. This short quote falls under "Fair Use" laws.)

Gov. Perry's spokesman stated that he had not seen the letter and could not comment on it. To be fair, the women involved did not make it easy for investigators. They would change their stated names between one investigator and the next, changed the children's names, traded children around, etc. making it almost impossible to determine which children were whose. Most had no birth certificates. Three hundred of the 416 children removed from the ranch were under four years old. Officials had difficulty determining whether some young mothers were over or under eighteen years of age and therefore legally adults. Even the lawyers for the children had difficulty with children and mothers "stonewalling." Lawyers who arrived in droves to represent children found that they had to meet with their clients in corners of the coliseum.

Officials finally had to separate mothers from their children. CPS defended this move by stating:

> "We believe that children who are victims of abuse of neglect, and particularly victims at the hands of their own parents, certainly are going to feel safer to tell their story when they don't have a parent there that's coaching them on how to respond. This is typical of any child protective case we work across the state of Texas every single day."

(Houston Chronicle, April 16, 2008, B-1 & 2. The author subscribes to the newspaper and retained the clipping from her copy. This short quote falls under "Fair Use" laws.)

> Later some of the women spoke, insisting that no woman is forced to remain at the ranch. They go from there to doctor's appointments, to visit relatives, etc. They claimed no girl is forced

into marriage. One stated that her two teen-aged daughters were not even thinking about marriage. But when asked if under-aged girls were allowed to be spiritually married, some of the women didn't seem to understand what "under-aged" meant. They also insisted that it was a free choice they made.

(Houston Chronicle, *April 17, 2008, B-1 & 5, paraphrased by the author. The author subscribes to the newspaper and retained the clipping from her copy. This short quote falls under "Fair Use" laws.*)

The first formal hearing dissolved into chaos. When Judge Barbara Walther took the bench, she was deluged with a storm of objections and motions from 250 attorneys about everything from the fact that all the cases were to be heard at one time to whether an investigator could read from her notes. One observer stated that the judge seemed to be doing an unbelievable job handling the mess. Ultimately, the judge decided in favor of CPS and ruled that the children would remain in state custody for at least six more weeks because "evidence proved they were at risk of abuse. . . until each child be granted individual hearings by June 5."

(Houston Chronicle, *April 19, 2008, A-1, paraphrased by the author. The author subscribes to the newspaper and retained the clipping from her copy. This short quote falls under "Fair Use" laws.*)

Betty Luke, a South Texas College of Law professor called the two day hearing an "ugly side." "There was no meaningful way to have my client addressed at this cattle call . . . There has been no way yet to meaningfully represent my client." She also had difficulty reaching a CPS caseworker.

(Houston Chronicle, *April 24, 2009, A-8, paraphrased by the author. The author subscribes to the newspaper and retained the clipping from her copy. This short quote falls under "Fair Use" laws.*)

By April 22, it was reported that Texas Rangers had reason to think the original anonymous phone call that led to the removal of the children might have been made not by a girl within the compound, but by a woman in Arizona who had been studying the sect for a long time and had made similar calls before pretending to be a teen girl in the sect's Arizona group. Her activities were reported to be an effort to help young women escape from the sect. This led to legal arguments about whether there was enough probable cause for the removal. Lawyers tended to get mixed up between family law (in which an anonymous call is enough probable cause to require CPS to investigate allegations) and criminal law (where an anonymous call would not be enough evidence of a crime to allow prosecution). At that same time, officials began to do DNA testing to determine which of the sect's children specifically belonged to what mothers and fathers. The judge had to order the parents to undergo these tests.

As stated, the initial removal had been initiated by an anonymous phone call. But on April 24, 2008, the *Houston Chronicle* reported that

> two prepaid mobile phones which had been used to make calls
> the previous month to a domestic violence shelter in San Angelo
> had been used before by one woman in calls to abuse hot lines
> in Colorado and Washington. This thirty-three-year-old woman
> had pleaded guilty in June, 2007, to false reporting and was
> placed on probation. She had been charged the previous week in
> Colorado for misdemeanor false reporting to authorities there.
> Jim Harrington, director of Texas Civil Rights Project said that
> the fact that the state launched this removal of children on what
> appeared to be a hoax tip without checking it out made a "sham"
> out of constitutional protections against wrongful searches.

(Houston Chronicle, *April 24, 2008, B-1, paraphrased by the author. The author subscribes to the newspaper and retained the clipping from her copy. This short quote falls under "Fair Use" laws.)*

The sheriff of the county in which San Angelo is located had been quoted as saying that the hot line call had been "essential" to obtaining the search warrant.

(*Houston Chronicle*, April 25, 2008, A-6, paraphrased by the author. The author subscribes to the newspaper and retained the clipping from her copy. This short quote falls under "Fair Use" laws.)

------◆◆◆◆------

While mothers who were breast-feeding their infants were allowed to remain with their children, other children were shipped off in droves to various group homes around the state from the panhandle to Southeast Texas, with groups going to Brazoria, Montgomery, and Harris Counties. While there were no plans then to make the children available for adoption, some siblings were widely separated even though officials did attempt to keep siblings together. This caused further problems for their parents to try to have "supervised" visits, since they had to travel from San Angelo, to the panhandle area and clear down to Houston with many hours of driving between locations. CPS had to change its total count of children removed as it found that some women thought to be adults were in fact under age eighteen.

The Austin-based Third Court of Appeals agreed to consider arguments from a group of mothers who wanted the state to provide evidence on a child-by-child basis, overturning Judge Walther's decision to keep all of the children in state custody after only generalized evidence had been presented. Robert Doggett, a legal aid representing about forty-eight mothers said he would ask the appeals court to order individual hearings for the children in the counties where they were placed in foster care.

Complicating matters further was the fact that "one young mother told investigators that she was fifteen when she gave birth to her first child. Texas law prohibits children under sixteen from being married. CPS investigators said those practices put all girls at risk of sexual abuse and all boys at risk of becoming men who abuse minor girls."

(Houston Chronicle, April 25, 2006, A-6, paraphrased by the author. The author subscribes to the newspaper and retained the clipping from her copy. This short quote falls under "Fair Use" laws.)

Days went by. One teen mother gave birth to a son. Authorities argued about how many girls were pregnant. People in general responded to the needs of the children donating school clothes, backpacks, diapers, etc. Every day another article appeared in the *Houston Chronicle*, some showing the "advantage" to the sect parents and some decrying those parents. One day would bring stories of children with old bone fractures and possible abuse of boys, and the next day another story would refute the previous day's reporting. The media were having a field day and costs to the state for the kids in custody and lawyers rose to ten million dollars.

Columnists had plenty of fodder for the op-ed section and their opinions went both ways from stating that the welfare of children must come first to calling the ranch where the sect lived a "pedophile ring."

(Ellen Goodman's column in the Houston Chronicle *on May 18, 2008, E-3, paraphrased by the author. The author subscribes to the newspaper and retained the clipping from her copy. This short quote falls under "Fair Use" laws.)*

CPS was under a new level of scrutiny in the case against Yearning for Zion parents. Most child abuse cases don't make headline news across the nation. Most individual families fighting to get their children back do not have the financial resources to hire the best lawyers that the parents of this separatist Mormon sect had. Never before had a case involved so many children at once. Blogs and talk radio hammered at their actions from both sides, some in support of CPS efforts to protect the children and others condemning them and supporting the parents' rights even though many of those same people did not support polygamy or under-age marriages. (This writer falls into the category of supporting the parents' rights while not believing in polygamy or under-age marriage.)

Perhaps the thorniest issue was whether to consider the children all as one family (in which the theory goes that if one child has been abused, all are "at risk") or as multiple families (in which case only those families with teen mothers, children in their teens or about to become teens would be considered "at risk"). CPS had chosen the "one household" theory based on the fact that there were several teen mothers and some children had told them that they considered all adults at the ranch their "parents" and all children their "siblings." On the opposing side were the lawyers for the children who stated that the "one household" theory did not allow each child a fair hearing and, further, they could not adequately represent the best interests of each child. Some parents at the ranch lived in monogamous relationships, had no criminal records, and had never abused their children in any way. Others argued for multiple households on the basis that while members of the group were polygamists, they were very rigid when it came to determining who is in which family. CPS had to concede that the case of "baby Jessop" which had named "Sarah" as the mother and Jessop, one of the sect's leaders, as father, must be dropped since it had been proven that "Sarah" did not exist and the original anonymous call had been a hoax.

A status hearing was held on May 19, 2008, during which CPS had to report progress on the case(s) to the judge, give parents their "family service plans," which would outline what parents had to do to get their children back. CPS did state that the goal of the case(s) was to reunite families after being reassured by parents that they would protect their daughters from under-age marriages, conditions under which parents could visit their children, etc. These hearings were projected to last some three weeks. In the time between the original removal and the status hearings, two more children had been born and several "disputed adults" had been proven to be over eighteen.

Criticism of CPS began immediately over "family service plans" that were vague, broad and short on specifics, making them almost impossible to complete. "This plan is so broad, my client has no idea what she's to do now," Donna Guion, attorney for Sharon Barlow, stated. Barlow's son was one of ten children in CPS custody belonging to Jeffs, who had been convicted in Utah as an accomplice to rape for forcing a fourteen-year-old girl to marry a nineteen-year-old man. Other parents complained that they had no input into the plans drafted just hours before the hearings. Several parents refused to sign the plans stating they were unworkable and impossible to complete. One attorney described the plans as designed by someone in Austin who had never met the children or their parents.

> "The agency defended what FLDS (Fundamentalist Church of Latter Day Saints) spokesman Rod Parker called 'cookie cutter' plans, insisting the plans are merely a starting point for both sides."

(Houston Chronicle, *May 20, 2008, B-4. The author subscribes to the newspaper and retained the clipping from her copy. This short quote falls under "Fair Use" laws.)*

Attorneys continued to argue over the next few days that the plans did not include any proof about how a parent had harmed each individual child.

Recall the statements earlier about our family's service plan. I had no access, of course, to any of those families' Service Plans, but I would bet that they were identical to ours except for parent names. The odds would definitely be in favor of my bet.

On May 22, 2008, CPS attempted to enter Yearning for Zion ranch because they had been told other children had arrived there since the initial removal. Guy Jessop stood guarding the gate and refused to let them enter unless they had a warrant. The two CPS workers were accompanied by a sheriff's deputy but left, admitting they did not have a warrant. They returned later and spoke to Jessop again. "For me to say there are no children here, I cannot," he told them, adding that children had come from other states to visit relatives there. "How many other children are going to be taken out of here if they happen to be visiting their grandmothers?" Jessop wondered aloud.

(Houston Chronicle, May 22, 2998, B-1 &5, paraphrased by the author. The author subscribes to the newspaper and retained the clipping from her copy. This short quote falls under "Fair Use" laws.)

This is not to say the sect was "innocent" of all charges against them. Carolyn Jessop had come to Texas to help train foster parents and others dealing with the children. She told of her own experiences being raised in the cult. Carolyn's mother had been taken in a raid on the sect's community in Short Creek, Arizona, in 1953. That raid ended in public backlash and the sect rebuilt its community there. Jessop had been born in Utah where her family had practiced polygamy for six generations. Her father had married her off at age eighteen to Merrill Jessop who was thirty-two years older than she and already had three other wives. Carolyn fled her home in Colorado City, Arizona, in 2003, and had published a book, *Escape*, about her experiences.

(Houston Chronicle, May 23, 2008, A-8, paraphrased by the author. The author subscribes to the newspaper and retained the clipping from her

Ms. Jessop was addressing a group of foster care and social workers on the finer points of handling children from the sect (considerations such as not wearing red because the sect believes that would be mocking Christ because red is reserved for Christ alone) when the word came that the 3rd Court of Appeals in Austin had ruled that the state had had no right to seize the hundreds of children and that the state had failed to prove they were in immediate danger of abuse. The appeals court judge ruled that the San Angelo judge had exceeded her authority in ordering all the children into foster care, not just the teenage girls who CPS said were at risk of being sexually abused by marriages to older men arranged by the sect.

> Parents of sect children rejoiced, but Ms. Jessop's reaction was, "I just can't believe they are just sending them back. That everyone can pretend that the abuse didn't happen."

Not that the Appeals Court ruling ended the matter. CPS and its umbrella agency immediately appealed to the Texas Supreme Court to overturn the Appeals Court ruling. Lawyers for the children and the parents compiled papers stating a number of legal errors on the part of CPS:

- "Insufficient investigation of the initial tip and tipster.
- Insufficient investigation at the ranch about who was in immediate danger.

- Treating the entire compound as one household, though there were nineteen separate residences.
- Taking all children instead of just the post-pubescent girls who could have been subjected to sexual abuse by older men.
- Insufficient evidence presented at the first hearing for the children.
- The hearing should have been for each individual child, not all in one hearing.
- Shifting the burden of proof to parents to prove innocence, rather than having CPS prove guilt."

(Houston Chronicle, May 25, 2008, B-4, paraphrased by the author. The author subscribes to the newspaper and retained the clipping from her copy. This short quote falls under "Fair Use" laws.)

The Texas State Supreme Court also ruled in favor of the parents: that removing all the children was not justified. During the summer months, most children were allowed to return to their parents and homes. Proceeding on a case-by-case basis, CPS did file separate motions to remove some children from their parents again and did prosecute a few of the men for sexual abuse. The *Houston Chronicle* reported on four petitions by the state to place eight FLDS children back in foster care on August 6, 2008.

Other repercussions continued for many months. An August 27, 2008, article in the *Houston Chronicle* stated that CPS workers feared the Mormon sect case would make it more difficult for them to protect children who were truly in danger of being abused. Memos went out to all caseworkers outlining new requirements to be met before a child was removed from a home. The state/CPS would have to obtain parental consent or a court order prior to removal "unless life or limb is in immediate jeopardy or sexual abuse is about to occur." Investigators would also have to weigh factors for each child living in a home before removing any of them based on allegations of abuse involving another child.

(Houston Chronicle, *Aug. 27, 2008, A-6, paraphrased by the author. The author subscribes to the newspaper and retained the clipping from her copy. This short quote falls under "Fair Use" laws.)*

By October of 2008, CPS had ended monitoring of all but thirty-seven of the sect's children. This meant that the state could still watch over these children and step in if conditions showed the parents might not continue to protect their children from under-age marriages.

A year later, CPS released some reports on the case and stated that only the number of children involved made the FLDS case any different from thousands of cases the state handles each year. Terry Langford of the *Houston Chronicle* did not feel the same way. "One year later, it's clear that the investigation, which ballooned into the nation's largest child custody case, was anything but typical."

"From the enormous time and money spent—more than 12 million in taxpayer dollars on everything from foster care and genetic testing to security, hotels, transportation and overtime pay for hundreds of state workers—CPS workers determined that twelve teen girls had been sexually abused by marrying adult members of the Fundamentalist Church of Jesus Christ of Later Day Saints."

(Houston Chronicle, *March 29, 2009, B-1, paraphrased by the author. The author subscribes to the newspaper and retained the clipping from her copy. This short quote falls under "Fair Use" laws.)*

Several other differences set the case apart as well. Sect members had access to better than average legal counsel valued at over $100 million to fight the state agency. They quickly used cameras, the media and the internet to plead their case even though they wear nineteenth century dress. Sect members also effectively used the argument that the state's raid on their compound was only a tool to persecute them for their religious beliefs. The fact that their life style was so different that processed foods actually made some children ill and the problem of figuring out family relationships in a group that had intermarried for generations made identifying "which family they belonged to, defied any Texas legal playbook." The fact that the original raid was based on a phone call that proved to be a hoax made it more difficult for later criminal investigations that require more evidence. While the sect quickly agreed to end their practice of underage marriages—the main victory of CPS, and rightly so—there may not be a way to make sure that the sect keeps that promise.

(Houston Chronicle, March 29, 2009, B-4, paraphrased by the author. The author subscribes to the newspaper and retained the clipping from her copy. This short quote falls under "Fair Use" laws.)

In April of 2009, several sect members appeared before a Texas State House of Representatives committee considering new legislation that would extend the statute of limitations for bigamy and increase criminal penalties for people who fail to report child abuse. Sect members claimed the new law would target them unfairly. State legislators sought a way to make sure children were sufficiently protected.

(Austin American Statesman, April 15, 2009, B1 & 10, paraphrased by the author from a clipping of that newspaper sent to the author by a friend who lives in Austin.)

And so the argument continues.

———•━•━•———

To me, it is important that the argument does continue. All these cases point out that in Texas, and in many other states, "the system" is broken and in great need of overhaul. Only continued discussion and true soul searching will help states, and our nation, find the proper balance between any state's duty to protect children and the rights of individual parents and families not to be interfered with unnecessarily.

The cases discussed in this book are only a few that might have been included. There were many times over the course of our family's experience that someone would tell us about a family they knew who had been through a CPS case. Most of these were not included because I was unable to talk directly to the people involved, or they did not wish to discuss their cases with me. There were a few times when I could not decide whether people were being honest with me or not. If I had any doubts, I felt I should not report on that case.

PART III

Recommendations for Improving the System

Recommendations for Improving the System

T he system" has a dismal failure rate both with innocent families and with children who die in abusive situations because they were not found in time or because CPS failed to see the seriousness of a situation and did not remove a child from an abusive home. While no human system will ever be perfect, the current situation must be changed. Children's Protective Services must be held more accountable. Yet parents must have their legal rights protected as well.

I noted many times over the twenty-three years of my full-time teaching career that politicians and people in power often called for drastic changes in the educational system. Rarely, however, did they ask people who worked in the field what they thought should be done. Those of us who were in the classroom every day were rarely, if ever, asked for our opinion on needed changes in education.

In a similar way, caseworkers, lawyers and those in law enforcement are the best people to ask what types of changes are needed for Children's Protective Services. I sought out several such people. Most did not return my calls, but a few agreed to speak with me. Some said I could use their names, while others requested to remain anonymous.

A report by the Texas Home School Coalition and Association in their 2008-09 *Handbook for Home Schoolers* stated that families who home school their children often seemed to be the targets of anonymous phone calls to CPS. The association devoted an entire chapter to the subject. They reported receiving a letter from CPS that the agency did not consider home schooling to be a risk to the safety of children and confirmed this in a memo to CPS staff.

The THSC also posted practical tips for families in the event that a caseworker should show up at a family's home asking to come in or interview their children. With their permission, I quote the following:

> "The CPS Worker at Your Door"
> - Record any conversation or interview with a CPS worker, using audio or video recording devices. (We recommend this to ensure that you can later prove what was said and by whom.)
> - When you begin recording, state your name and the date and ask each person involved to give their name and title as well.
> - Stay calm.
> - Be polite and friendly. Smile.
> - Get the social worker's business card.
> - Do not let him into your home. The only legal ways into your home are with: emergency situation (immediate and obvious danger to life of limb); your permission; or a search warrant.
> - Do not allow him to interview your children.
> - Tell him you are willing to cooperate if he will tell you what the charges are.
> - When he tells you, tell him you will take your child(ren) to your physician and have him write a report to CPS.
> - Repeat the above statements as often as necessary. Do not be afraid of silence.

- After he leaves, write down everything that occurred and call THSC at 806-774-4441 and/or your attorney."

(Handbook for Texas Home Schoolers, 2008-2009, Texas Home School Coalition Association, PO Box 6747, Lubbock, TX, 79493, www.THSC.org, 2008, pages 2-12 and 2-13. Quoted with permission.)

I might add to that:

* Families should examine every detail of any allegation against them.

Even when parents are distraught and stressed to the max, they should pay careful attention to small details on any document. Had we noticed the discrepancy in the dates on our original affidavit, we might have saved ourselves months of heartache.

------●-•-●------

CPS Supervisor, Ms. 246, spoke with me by phone concerning her work in a rural/small town area. I asked her first what factors helped her region be mostly successful with their cases. Her response indicated that early involvement with a family was one key. The sooner her caseworkers were able to step in and become involved in helping a family through a time of crisis, or other situation, the better the chances of keeping that family together (no removal of children to foster care or placement with relatives needed) and of keeping the children involved safe. Another point she made was that, for the most part, the same caseworker stayed with a family throughout their case. Caseworkers got to know families very well and were able to sense when things might be taking a turn for the worse. The only time a family was handed off to a different caseworker was when the current caseworker left the agency. A new worker might also be assigned if the court released a family from supervision and then later the family came back into the system, but the new worker could easily check with the former caseworker. Ms. 246 also mentioned that her area was fortunate in that it did not have a high turn-over rate among employees.

I asked if she encountered cases in which an ex-spouse, boyfriend/girlfriend wrongfully reported their former wife/ husband, boyfriend/girlfriend for child abuse on their anonymous tip line. She said that it did happen quite frequently and that they always investigated within forty-eight hours. Because she knows her caseworkers well, and they know their clients well, and the agency knows, generally speaking, what problems there are around the area (small towns know what's going on in people's lives more often than they do in urban areas) the caseworker could ask around pretty quickly and "screen out" such false reports. She said if a caseworker found out that a parent was working steadily, had children in a licensed daycare facility, and their home was relatively clean (she doesn't see a problem with an occasionally cluttered home and dishes in a sink) the caseworker will quickly drop that case.

When asked if there should be some sort of penalty for "malicious" false reports, she reported that she didn't think filing a lawsuit against an angry "ex" would really help. For one thing, the prosecutors and courts in her area probably would not want to waste their time on such an effort. Also, if that "ex" is providing child support and you put that person in jail, then they can't provide the money needed for the children. Mrs. 246 thought some type of "fair warning citation" might work better.

The average length of CPS involvement with a family was six months. Some cases were resolved in as little as three months, but when the family already had a history of problems, or when parents had drug/alcohol problems, then it might take six months, a year or longer to get the family back on the right track.

The biggest problems Ms. 246 had were with local judges who, according to her, seemed to be more concerned with dollars and the cost of putting/keeping a child in foster care.

"There are some people you just can't fix, and I feel it is better to err on the side of caution with those parents," she said. But the judges in her area were often reluctant to remove children from the home, or they would remove one child and leave siblings. "Obviously, if one child is affected, the others will be. Or if one teenager in a family has become involved with drugs, and there are other teenagers or pre-teens, the odds are pretty good those kids will become involved, too. Sometimes there doesn't seem to be any common sense. A judge may want to keep a child in the home because the budget is short, or they get too caught up in trying to fix the parent and do not focus on the child. Many times, the children need more counseling and mentoring than we give them. If the child doesn't get good counseling and mentoring, they simply grow up to become abusers and the cycle keeps going." More emphasis is needed on breaking that cycle.

Heavy case loads are always a problem. Her state had recently made changes to reduce case loads to an ideal of four to five cases per worker with a maximum of ten, but in reality, that doesn't happen often. Her workers alternate weekends and try to relieve each other to alleviate some of the high stress involved with the job, but it doesn't always work the way it should.

Ms. 246 felt that in many ways, "We have created this monster." Besides the obvious needs of more money and manpower, the keys seemed to her to be:

- Not being focused on how much money it costs to have a child in foster care.
- Focus less on "fixing the parent" (some people can't or won't be "fixed") and focus more on the

child's needs to grow up with healthy attitudes there-by breaking the cycle for the next generation.

- Caseworkers should get to know their clients better. "Lifetime assignment" of caseworker to family would be great—that worker would know what to look for. While in reality one "lifetime" worker may not be possible, it would be a worthy goal to strive for.

After thanking Ms. 246 for her time, I thought about how different it might have been for our family if we had had the same caseworker throughout, instead of the Harris County system of automatically having multiple workers one "intake," one "investigative," and one or more "service" workers. I never even met some of the caseworkers assigned to our case. A couple, I only talked to on the phone once.

Because Ms. 246 must stand in front of the same judges she criticizes to advocate for other children, I will not reveal in what state she lives and works except to say that it is not Texas.

—•◦•—

Linda Sanchez (who stated it would be fine with her to use her name) works for Good Will Farm, a private social agency in Michigan. Working with this private agency is different from working with the state. There are not as many problems in her experience. But she does work in conjunction with Michigan's Department of Human Services (DHS). Her job is placing children in private foster care if the state does not have foster families available. She also works with foster families, providing training, helping navigate the system, helping the children adjust who are placed in their care, etc.

Another of her duties is licensing homes for foster care, doing home studies, and writing up reports. Sanchez is a Supervisor for her agency, in charge of caseworkers and foster homes. The DHS frequently calls her agency and says saying something like, "We need a place for a five-year-old. Do you have any families available?" She then takes over the case and the State appoints a monitor to that case so they can also keep track of the child. This "outsourcing" lessens the state's paperwork and the burden on the state's foster care system. DHS only places children with Good Will Farms when they can't find a family in their own system.

Sanchez Follows the same rules and procedures as the state, but many of Good Will's rules are more stringent than those of the State of Michigan. Many children have already gone through Michigan's system and may have developed additional problems as a result. Sanchez's caseworkers go to court with and for children placed with them, and follow through with any other programs set up to help these children.

Linda Sanchez has also been a foster parent herself. She has seen children sent home when she didn't think a parent had really changed, become more responsible, or was ready to have their child back. That, to her, was heartbreaking.

"People have the idea that it's the DHS that returns kids to homes, but they only make recommendations to the Court. So much depends on the judge. Some judges send kids home too soon and others don't. Each case can be so different."

She stated that, in general, in Michigan, Children's Protective Services can't remove a child from a home without giving evidence to the Court. A lot of these kids are already on DHS "radar." Exactly when a child is removed from the home depends in part on who reported the case to authorities. For instance, a doctor in a hospital or a police officer in an emergency can have a child removed immediately if they are on scene and there seems to be domestic violence. Rarely is a child removed from a home without just cause. (I wondered if our situation would have occurred in Michigan.)

Sanchez reported that Michigan had recently settled a lawsuit that might have bankrupted the system because of a few cases of bad foster care. The suit was brought by a child advocacy group. There have been many changes as a result of the suit such as lowering case loads (more home visits, etc.) because a child died while in foster care. In another case, a child adopted by foster parents later died at the hand of those adoptive parents. Sanchez feels these changes are for the better in the protection of children in the system.

Linda Sanchez does, however, see problems remaining. She also sees a lot of families with alcoholism, parents who are partying all the time, and not adequately caring for their children. In the area where she works, there is a high rate of alcoholism and it is generational. Parents have that "it was good enough for me, and it's good enough for my kids" attitude. Sanchez disagrees with such parents.

She often feels parents are given multiple chances to shape up (especially when it comes to drugs and alcohol). There seem to be no consequences for a "dirty test," and often asks, "Why is that parent out on the streets?" Often, parents only shape up when they are close to having their rights terminated. Sanchez feels the system doesn't hold these parents responsible enough for their behavior, and kids are the ones hurting. She has had many experiences where the children think they are the ones being punished after all, their parents got to stay home while they are out with strangers.

There are days Linda is a strong advocate for the idea that people should have to pass a test and obtain a license to have a baby. "Just like you have to pass a test to get a license to drive a car," although this may not be practical.

Another aspect of the greater problem is the huge number of teen-age girls having babies who are not at all prepared for the huge responsibility of parenthood.

When I asked for some ideas about improving the system, she mentioned these points:

- "The earlier we start teaching parenting skills the better, and not just teaching abstinence in sex education classes, but teaching young people how to protect themselves from STDs, how not to have babies, etc. More early childhood education would be better, too."

- She sees that kids are not in the foster care system for as long a time as they used to be. The system is supposed to be about reunification of families, and many times that does work. She noted that permanency hearings usually take place within one year now not the three or four years as often happened previously. "Get kids home; or sever the parents' rights," she stated. "Parents are held more accountable than in the past."

- The biggest positive thing she has seen in her state is that now, when kids come into the system and are placed with relatives, that relative must go through the process to become a foster parent. (Sometimes in years past, when a child was placed with Aunt So-and-so, that child might be in just as much danger they were with the parent.) But now, in ninety percent of relative placement cases, the relatives do become foster parents and receive proper training. Grandparents who become foster parents can now receive financial compensation from the State of Michigan as foster parents. This helps a lot of people who could not otherwise accept fostering a grandchild. Older couples saddled with care of a grandchild may find their fixed incomes and greater expenses quite strained.

- Good Will Farm caseworkers must do home visits twice a month and call twice a month, not just one visit and two calls a month as state caseworkers do. This provides foster parents with much more support and help with handling sometimes difficult children. They also arrange respite care so foster parents experience less burn-out. Her agency wants to do an even better job than her state does.

After this discussion with Linda, I felt that the State of Texas would be wise to adopt some of the same policies regarding better investigation before a child is removed from a home, case loads, home visits, and monetary support for relatives fostering children. It is sad that it took a law suit against the State of Michigan by a child advocacy group to accomplish these reforms.

———

Randy Burton founded an organization called Justice for Children and is a partner in the law firm of Burleson Cooke, LLP, in Houston, Texas. On Aug. 16, 2009, the *Houston Chronicle* ran an editorial piece in the Sunday "Outlook" section written by him after yet another child died at the hands of an abusive live-in boyfriend and the mother failed to protect her child. I spoke with Mr. Burton on the phone on August 21, 2009, and asked him more about his opinions. He stated quite clearly that he feels that in Harris County, Texas, CPS does not have funding issues or manpower issues. His most important point was to say that CPS should **not** be the agency to investigate allegations of child abuse. He graciously gave me permission to quote from his editorial article.

> "CPS Under Fire in Death of Emma"
> "Law Enforcement Should Investigate Crimes against Children"
>
> "The death of 4-year old Emma Thompson has enraged the Houston Community. . . Houstonians have reserved their strongest criticism for Child Protective Services. The agency, which was fully aware that Emma had contracted a sexually transmitted disease, failed to remove her from the home.
>
> "This tragedy is not an isolated example of poor judgment but the result of a conscious decision by CPS to leave this child in the home. CPS spokesperson Estella Olguin explained that 'a sexually transmitted disease alone is not enough to put a 4-year-old into protective custody.'
>
> "In May 1987, following the murder of 2-year-old Jesse Wheeler . . . Justice for Children was formed by a group of concerned citizens tired of seeing preventable deaths of very young children in our community.
>
> "Later that year, these same Houstonians convinced the Texas Senate to conduct statewide hearings into the problems at CPS. The 1989 Senate report stated that '70 percent of the confirmed cases involved children who were left in their homes and who needed ongoing supervision and assistance from the department. In reality, only about half of these cases were assigned to a caseworker. The remaining 49 percent, or 9,800 confirmed cases, were closed immediately after the investigation . . .'
>
> "In 1991, the Texas Senate Finance Committee found that . . . 'the immense problems and substantial improvements required cannot be achieved realistically in an agency with so many competing priorities.'
>
> "Also in 1991, a report by the Texas Performance Review Team found: 'The mission of the social worker is to rehabilitate and preserve the family. . . On the other hand, the mission of an investigator is to determine if the abuse occurred and remove

the victim from the situation if necessary. Maintain-ing the functions in the same agency makes . . . a nearly impossible situation in which to maintain objectivity and focus.'

"On July 2, 2004, Gov. Rick Perry issued an executive order requiring the Office of the Inspector General of the Texas Health and Human Services Commission to conduct an investigation of CPS. The inspector general's report noted that: 'When abuse or neglect was indicated in the file, only 30 percent of the time did CPS caseworkers implement the appropriate safety steps for short term protection of the child, only 71 percent of the time were steps appropriate to protect the child from further abuse and neglect and only 27 percent of the time, when there was imminent threat to the health and safety of any child in the home, was the child actually removed from the threat to prevent further abuse, neglect, or physical abuse, neglect, or physical harm to the child.'

"Twenty-three years after Jesse Wheeler's death, innumerable studies, and adverse reports, we are still fighting the same fight. I could not care less that CPS feels they are damned if they remove a child and damned if they don't. . . Of the one million annual cases where CPS confirmed abuse and neglect, 72 percent were closed without ever removing the children. By comparison, the number of children who have been murdered as a result of being removed from a home subsequently deemed safe is a big fat zero. . .

"CPS is not required to use reasonable efforts to keep families together where 'the parent has subjected the child to . . . abandonment, torture, chronic abuse and sexual abuse' or 'has committed a felony assault that results in serious bodily injury to a child.'

"No government agency is perfect, but I'd much rather have a police officer investigate a crime against a child than the agency that acknowledges that it doesn't perform criminal investigations. Law enforcement's priority is to protect its complaining witness, the crime victim. Otherwise, it has no case. CPS's priority continues to be preserving the family unit which, in cases like Emma's is an experiment at the child's expense."

(*Houston Chronicle*, Sunday, August 16, 2009, section B11, used with the telephone permission of Mr. Burton.)

———————

I stopped to think about what might have happened in our case if a police officer had been the one to investigate. The officer might still have decided to remove our grandson from his parents since James did have a head injury. However, that police officer would have been obligated to investigate our side of the story as well. I seriously doubt that it would have taken thirteen months for the police department (and accompanying forensic lab) to view James's February 20, 2007, CT scan to see that the seizures, not the injury, occurred first. I also believe a police officer would have looked at the rest of Texas Childrens Hospital's records and noted that on that fateful night, James had **not one** other bruise anywhere on his body. That officer would probably have come to the common sense realization that abusive parents most likely do not hit their children in only one place. A police investigator would probably have completed a thorough investigation during the time James was in the hospital and have completed it by the time he was ready to be released, or at least in less than the thirteen months it took CPS to come to the conclusion that they should "non-suit" our case.

———————

In 2005, the Texas Legislature wrote a law that began a program in that state to hire "special investigators" who did have police backgrounds to work with Children's Protective Services in that state. An in-depth article by Terri Langford on this program appeared in the *Houston Chronicle* on Oct. 12, 2009. Some of the main points of that article follow.

"Since then [2005] 431 special investigators have been hired by CPS, 273 have left the agency" for a variety of reasons. "Today, the concept seems to have run aground as more than a third of the state's 236 positions sit vacant." . . .

"The SI program's apparent shortfalls come at a critical time as the agency confronts even more scrutiny over flawed investigations following four child abuse deaths. In fact, not one of those cases was assigned a special investigator." . . .

"State officials reasoned four years ago that hiring law enforcement veterans and putting them to work at CPS would not only save more lives but perhaps infect the agency with better and more modern tracking techniques." . . .

"According to SIs who left, the program's goals were muddled from the start. Some ex-SIs said they assumed they would eventually be gun-toting officers for the agency, something CPS officials insist was never in the cards. But the position's fuzzy definition helped exacerbate the inevitable culture clash between social workers and police officers. . . .

"'Police officers are pretty hard-nosed about things. They see things in black and white' said Steven Ray Rogers, 68, of Weatherford, who worked as a special investigator for 19 months before leaving last summer. 'The very nature of their job is to infringe on people's freedom.' CPS workers, on the other hand, are college-educated and tend to be younger and less experienced with troubled domestic relationships. They are not only asked to evaluate the evidence before them, but to make educated guesses about future behavior of parents." . . .

"Also, every decision about a child's welfare must be reviewed with a supervisor. 'It wasn't the job I was led to believe,' said Thomas Davidson, a 40-year veteran of law enforcement who worked for CPS in Houston for two months in 2007. 'It's more of a caseworker than an investigator (job)'" Davidson, who also is a former foster parent, quickly found CPS' culture, where caseworkers must get every child removal and placement approved, frustrating. 'You had to say 'Mother may I' to four different supervisors,' the 68 year old recalled. 'That's not exactly what I had in mind.'" . . .

Keith Jemison, 35, who left CPS after six weeks and is now chief of the Montgomery ISD police force stated, "You were being supervised by someone with no law enforcement experience and you're supposed to be advising that person and they see you as a glorified case worker." . . .

Another quote read, "You had two different cultures, two different communities converging, law enforcement and social work, in a social work setting with its awesome responsibilities, but not the powers and authority associated with law enforcement." . . .

"Some former SIs said CPS caseworkers had the information to solve a case, but because of the immense caseloads, they didn't always see it. . . Not all of the experiences were negative, though. Gary Hooper, 53, who worked for the Seguin office form 2006 to 2008 had high praise for his supervisors, and said he believes every officer should have to do it and the program should continue. 'It'd do everybody good to do the social services side. It will benefit you when you deal with families as a police officer.'"

(Houston Chronicle, Monday, Oct. 12, 2009, pg. A-1 and A-6, paraphrased by the author. The author subscribes to the newspaper and retained the clipping from her copy. This short quote falls under "Fair Use" laws.)

If enough heads came together in a good "think tank," perhaps a better partnership might be formed between social workers and law enforcement that would blend the skills of both and protect children while respecting the rights of parents with some presumption of innocence until proven guilty.

———————

Another article on December 15, 2009, summarized the findings of a report by the Texas Department of Family and Protective Services reviewing a randomly chosen ninety-five cases.

The major findings were stated as follows:

- Investigators failed to consider family's past CPS history in about half the cases.
- Many cases lacked attempts to contact the absent parent of the child abuse victim.
- Cases were transferred too quickly from investigators to family caseworkers.
- Investigators and family caseworkers failed to evaluate a child's risk adequately.

(Terri Langford, Houston Chronicle, Tuesday, Dec. 15, 2009, A-6, paraphrased by the author. The author subscribes to the newspaper and retained the clipping from her copy. This short quote falls under "Fair Use" laws.)

———•◦•◦•———

Ms. 56, who retired from CPS after thirty years as a dedicated case worker in an urban setting, had plenty to say about problems and fault on every side of every issue. Her wealth of information cast light on the problems since the 1970s when she began her career. While she did not feel afraid of talking to me *(What could they do to me now?)* I decided to stay on the safe side and not reveal her identity.

Our conversation began with her comments on problems within the CPS system. Many of the issues she discussed were not unexpected: Not enough workers; not enough foster parents; high turnover, people quitting every day, every month, walking out of training; too high case loads. "Case workers are so badly needed, but they have so little to work with. They need more workers, better pay, and a lower case load."

In addition, she said that in her area, case workers had no secretaries and had to do all their own paperwork, prepare for court dates, etc. During her career, caseworkers used their own vehicles to provide transportation for client families, children in care, etc. Caseworkers were reimbursed for mileage, but she felt agency should provide cars. When a case worker must drive a family or children in foster care around, it is necessary to have special liability insurance. Some caseworkers could not afford the necessary insurance for carrying other people. They might be "chancing it," transporting kids and parents without the extra insurance. If an accident happened, those people would already be mad at the state for taking their children away and would be very likely to sue the state or the caseworker personally. During Ms. 56's career, her state also cut back on the number of miles per month for which a caseworker could be reimbursed. There were times when a caseworker had to go over this limit, and then take on this expense from their limited salaries. Foster families, faced with the same budget limits, often would not transport children either, insisting that CPS take foster children to necessary doctor, dental, or psychological appointments.

Ms. 56 also saw problems with people who take in foster children. She said that some people think only of the money the state provides to keep kids. In spite of the fact that the amount received per child per month from her state is not very much, some people would manage to buy a new car or other luxury with that money. If you get enough kids, the amount grows. Some then spend it on themselves, not on the children in their care. "Also, if they get too many kids, they can't give proper attention to each. The state has no places for some of these kids." (I recalled a newspaper article I had seen during our experience with CPS in which it was stated that some children were sleeping in CPS offices temporarily.)

She said that her state loves a "free" home kinship care. But many other family members who might be willing to provide a home are single or elderly and on fixed income and they need more than the state provides in these instances. (This was similar to our family situation in Texas where we did not qualify for any help at all.)

The amount paid to foster parents had not kept up with

inflation. Kids can be picky eaters and that can run up the grocery bill. Anything and everything can go wrong. The money doesn't go far enough for most foster parents. As an example, she said that a family may have one "healthy" child, have another one going to therapy three times a week, and perhaps a third child where they don't know what's wrong. One may have been sexually abused, and may act this out through masturbation, or begin to abuse another of the foster children. Many foster parents in her state may not be properly trained to deal with such a situation. Problems then spread from one child to the next, and the family can't afford therapy for the other children from what they receive from the state.

Then there are the foster parents who become abusers themselves. She talked about one case she handled where several children of one mother were all in foster care but in different homes. As she returned the last little boy to his foster home after a supervised visit with his mother, the boy said, "I ain't going in there!" He was five. Until that moment, Ms. 56 had thought this boy could not talk. Pleased that he could talk, she asked him why. He had been with this foster mother for five months, and the foster mom had kept him in a playpen. He slept, played and ate in a play pen with a lid on it! The foster parent said she did that so he wouldn't mess up the house. Fortunately, she was able to place this boy with his siblings and shut down that foster home. The situation left Ms. 56 wondering, *Who does the state trust to keep these kids?* (I often wondered the same thing, considering it took nine months for CPS to do our "home study" that supposedly showed we were capable care-givers; yet, our grandson had been with us all that time before they investigated us.)

On the flip side, families who have their children taken away often do not do what they are supposed to do. Ms. 56 recalled many times one mother slept in the truck as Ms. 56 drove her to therapy or parenting classes. "This mother was still up all night out in bars abusing alcohol and drugs. Some mothers want to get away from their kids, or don't want them back at all, or they only want them back to get SSI benefits, which they then spend on themselves. Some parents even give up kids voluntarily. Many times, if the kids have been placed with a relative, and parents aren't supposed to see them, relatives let them see the kids anyway. Some mothers come to see their kids dressed to the hilt, enjoying life without them. There used to be a time when if you hit a kid, or a boyfriend beat up on a kid, grandmothers helped. Now some grandparents are on drugs, too. When parents won't do what they are supposed to do, what can CPS do?" she asked me.

She said she wonders about a screening process now when her state is so full and in such great need of foster parents that they can't be picky, and it's hard to get rid of bad foster parents. She was aware that some caseworkers were going to private providers, residential homes, etc., while others hired their own help.

I asked Ms. 56 if she recalled times when the system did work. She responded that back in the 1970s, when she first went to work for CPS, the agency wasn't as "big" and it did work. She said she had more personal contact with clients and families. She emphasized that it was **"not all state's fault, either,"** and that she has no faith in politicians to provide the funds necessary to do the job right in her state. She felt that a lot of agencies involved "are messed up."

"A lot depends on the caseworker you get. Some are good, some not. Some go by the book and some go way beyond." She told me she always wanted to know all about a family, and spend time with each. In an ideal situation, a caseworker would visit a child's parent, plus the child and foster parent weekly, but that is not possible most of the time. She stressed that we need more contact between the worker and the parent, and she felt that there are many times when too many chances are given to parents.

—•·•·•—

I took the advice of one friend and drove downtown to Houston's Juvenile Court building (I certainly knew how to get there and where the least expensive parking lot is located.) a few days and just sat on the seventh floor, observing and listening to the conversations going on around me. Ms. 56's comment about lots of talk and little really happening rang too true. I tried to sit close enough to the front to be able to hear more than I had on previous occasions. As various people stood before the presiding judge, I saw a lot of formality but little real action taken. Only occasionally did the presiding judge seem to do anything but rubber-stamp the CPS recommendation before him. Once I did hear a judge state that he had heard no evidence that a child should not be placed with his father. The judge ordered an expedited home study for the father and said the father should have the child by that Friday. (I was listening to this on a Tuesday.) I heard a lot of cases with a goal of relative adoption. I listened to one case in which a mother had three children, all with different fathers. One father was in jail, another was an alcoholic and the third couldn't be found. The mother in this case was admonished to stay on her alcoholic treatment program or face permanent severing of her rights to the children.

On one such occasion of listening in this manner, I was able to visit briefly with a lawyer on one of the cases. He stood by himself in the hallway outside the courtroom briefly and I was bold enough to approach and ask for a few minutes of his time. Mr. MM quickly agreed that "the system is terribly flawed." He went so far as to state that in Harris County, and he implied Texas in general, family courts and CPS cases are "an abortion clinic for separating children from their parents, especially if the families are poor, Black, or Hispanic." He felt that the rights of minority families were especially disregarded in the State of Texas and that perhaps it harkened back to the days before the Civil War when slave children were separated from their mothers, and mothers from the fathers of those children, and often sold away from each other as a way of destroying family ties and maintaining control.

"There was a day when Texas did not bastardize its children. If a parent had to relinquish parental rights, another family member, or other person with whom the child had already forged a relationship, was in Court the same day to take the child home. Usually, it was a person the natural parent had already approved. Now, some parents are forced to give up their rights, the child or children stay in foster care, and The State takes its time doing home studies on potential adoptive families. A parent giving up all rights may receive 'assurances' that CPS will turn their child over to family members or a friend the parent approved, but there are no 'guarantees' that CPS or The State will follow up in that manner."

Mr. MM had little he liked about "the system" as he saw it and worked hard to defend his clients whose children had landed in state custody. He compared the CPS system and its problems to the "stubborn ignorance" of Texans in the way they regard the sport of football and the ridiculously high salaries of professional players and the salaries of coaches even at the high school level. He wondered what good might come if school districts and universities spent as much on science as they did on football. Continuing that analogy, he felt that it might be a "good" thing ultimately that football salaries were so foolishly high because it would push that system into a cycle of collapse that would lead to change. Likewise, Children's Protective Services might also push itself in to a collapse that might lead to true reform.

For the sake of children, I hope he's right, and that change can't come soon enough.

———◦•✦•◦———

CPSIA information can be obtained at www.ICGtesting.com
Printed in the USA
237143LV00007B/5/P